M000305652

CONFESSIONS

of a

HOLLYWOOD
INSIDER:

*My Amusing Encounters
with The A-List*

SANDRO MONETTI

Published by: Hollywood International Film Exchange (Hi-Fex)
Cover photo by: Isaiah Mays
Cover design by: Eva Bian

Dedicated to: Virginia & Giorgio

Contents

INTRODUCTION

I've kissed Madonna, head-butted Tom Cruise, and peed on Samuel L. Jackson.

Such dubious achievements are all part of life when you're a Hollywood showbiz reporter and interviewer like me.

For as long as I can remember, I've been a starstruck fan of the celebrity world. I still am and can't believe my luck in getting to meet and report on so many talented idols.

As well as being a contributor to *CNN International* and the *BBC*, I talk about the entertainment business on a string of other TV and radio channels, interview stars for newspapers, magazines, podcasts, and books, introduce them at premieres and award shows, and host question and answer sessions with the biggest names on stage. How did I end up here? Like so many things, the answers can be found in childhood.

Growing up in England as an only child whose parents worked really hard as hoteliers, I spent a lot of time in front of the TV set, which became a kind of babysitter, friend, and teacher in those formative years as well an antidote to the mundanity of school. I was especially drawn to the escapism and adventure of the American shows and films, so my imaginary friends became the likes of *Captain Kirk, Knight Rider, The A-Team,* and *Rocky Balboa.*

A desire to draw closer to these famous icons and have a conversation with them grew in me. It was as if I wanted to climb into the television and be part of that world. I knew from an early age what career I wanted to pursue when I grew up: becoming a show business reporter, ideally in Hollywood.

That journalism career started on my hometown paper, Blackpool's *Evening Gazette*, and continued as columnist with much loved music magazine *Smash Hits* before working my way up to become a showbiz editor on various national UK newspapers in London. Then working for *Sky TV* first took me to the States where I launched a new chapter in my spiritual home in Hollywood. Along the way I took a brief detour into teaching, creating the world's first-degree course in celebrity journalism, wrote a couple of movie star biographies and plays, hosted a podcast, won a few reporting awards, and did many hundreds of star interviews, all with my signature look—wearing a smart suit, carrying a British flag bag, and with a beaming smile on my face.

No matter how hot L.A. gets, I always dress up for work—a lesson learned from Frank Sinatra to always respect your audience. I'll be dropping more names like that. And there is forever a big smile on my face. Why wouldn't there be? I love what I do and adore the city where I live.

Los Angeles was the first place in the world where I had truly felt at home—because from the moment I touched down in this sun-kissed dream factory, I recognized so many of the streets and buildings from the TV shows and movies I had always loved.

Plus, as someone pursuing his own ambitions, I related to the aspirational nature of the people. L.A. is a big shiny casino that works like a magnet to millions of dreamers. It's a special place which has given me magical memories, many of which I want to share with you in this book.

The key to interviewing is to make the guest the star and so this book is a collection of stories about well over a hundred idols I've interviewed, together with some things I learned from them along the way. Essentially it's a comedy book and I hope these stories make you smile even though many of them made me squirm.

I love interviewing celebrities and the question I'm most often asked when people hear that I've met just about every famous name is: what's (insert name of star here) really like? Well, by confessing my amusing encounters with the A-list, I hope you will find your answer in these pages.

My other hope is that your reaction to my work will be less painful than the one that greeted me when I was recognized during a showbiz party in the summer of 2019. While eagerly accepting some of the finger food being passed around on trays, I was approached by a rather angry looking fellow party guest.

He said, "I've seen you on CNN." But it seemed more like an accusation than a compliment.

I was about to thank him for watching and ask his name but before I could get the words out ... he kicked me firmly in the balls.

As I staggered back in pain, my attacker yelled triumphantly: "Fox News mother f---er!" Then ran off disappearing into the crowd.

I guess he wasn't a fan.

CHAPTER 1:
THE ICONS

SYLVESTER STALLONE

I thought it was the greatest night of my life … until I got a tap on the shoulder.

Looking through a curtain from backstage at England's Manchester Arena, I gazed out at five thousand excited fans waiting to see my life-long hero Sylvester Stallone about to be interviewed by me on stage. They chanted, "We want Rocky! We want Rocky!"

With one minute to go until I was to step onto that vast stage to introduce the action superstar, the show's promoter sheepishly asked for a word.

"Er, Sandro, bit of a problem, Sly's not here yet."

"You mean, he's not here at the theatre?"

"He's not even in Manchester."

"Where is he?"

"London."

"What's he doing there? That's hours away, we've got thousands of people out there chanting we want Rocky—and they want him now!"

"Can you fill?"

"Maybe for a few minutes, not for a few hours. I thought he was supposed to be flying into Manchester hours ago."

"He got on a later plane and apparently his people put him on a plane to London instead thinking England was so small it must be close by. Our driver picked him up and he's racing down the motorway now."

"Can we get him a police escort?"

"Tried that."

"What did the cops say?"

"This isn't Hollywood, mate."

"Fair point."

Scrambling for ideas, I suggested to the promoter we keep the crowd happy while waiting by giving them all a free drink and sticking the *Rocky IV* DVD on the big screen. He agreed to all that but still said I needed to go out there and explain the situation.

So I said I would, but first took a moment to figure out what I was going to say.

In that moment I remembered the previous time I'd met Sylvester Stallone, he was hours late then too!

It was in Las Vegas where I was due to interview him for a newspaper about his reality TV boxing series *The Contender*. After being made to wait for ages for our one-on-one interview, when it eventually happened Sly kept excusing himself every few minutes to "go and eat a protein pudding." It was part of his bodybuilding regime apparently.

He'd come back into the room and I'd ask, "How was the pudding?" He'd go, "Mmm, nice pudding" and then the chat would resume for a while until he excused himself again. Bizarre.

Now here I was, a couple of years later, and it was more than just me waiting for him, it was thousands of expectant fellow fans. As their chants grew louder and more impatient, I knew it was time to go out and break the news to them that we would all have to wait a bit longer.

Stepping on stage at the giant arena, I felt the excitement from this, the biggest crowd I had ever faced in my hosting career, and the dread of having to disappoint them. Time to stall, therefore I said … "Good evening, ladies and gentlemen, I'm your host Sandro Monetti (I paused for the smattering of applause). I know Sylvester Stallone's work means so much to every one of us. Me included. I was such a fan of his Rambo films that on my eighteenth birthday I flew from England to New York just for the day to see *Rambo 3* with an American audience. It remains the best birthday ever. The cinema crowd was so hyped up that when Sly was battling the Russian bad guys in the last twenty minutes, they left their seats, stood in a semicircle around the screen and chanted 'Ram-bo, Ram-bo!' What a memory."

The crowd was with me because they thought this was the preamble to me bringing him out on stage. I continued to stall….

"Tonight you're going to have a very special memory too. Sly will be on this stage answering my questions about *Rambo, Rocky, The Expendables,* and everything in between and then he'll take your questions from the audience. We'll sit on that sofa behind me where you see two microphones ready. We have members of the Royal Marines here to welcome him to the stage and first we'll show you on the big screen just why we love Stallone so much. Welcome to *An Evening with Sylvester Stallone*—it's an event worth waiting for….

"But we'll all have to wait just a bit longer as Sly is still in the car on the way to the venue so stay patient and see you soon…."

I raced from the stage to the sound of a few boos, jeers, and angrier chants of "We want Rocky."

An announcement over the loudspeaker of the free drinks calmed people down a little. So did watching *Rocky IV*—it is a great movie after all. I went to wait in Sylvester Stallone's plush dressing room—well he wasn't using it—and eventually, almost two hours after the show had been due to start, I got the call that Stallone's car was pulling up outside.

The Royal Marines had formed a guard of honor to welcome our star guest and the promoter was waiting ahead of them by the door to greet Stallone. He told me Sly had phoned from the car to say he needed half an hour to freshen up prior to going on stage. But I knew I couldn't leave the crowd waiting any longer without them tearing the place apart. Time to speak to the Marines….

Thinking he was used to receiving orders, I asked their commanding officer if on Stallone's arrival he would arrange for his men to march Stallone not through the door on the left which led to his dressing room but the one on the right that led to the stage. He agreed, thankfully, and so I got in position at the side of the stage.

Moments later to the surprise of many at Manchester Arena, mostly Sylvester Stallone himself, the Hollywood superstar was receiving a military escort onto the stage. I rushed on to introduce him and there was no escape for Sly who, feeling the warm embrace of the crowd, went with it and handled everything like a pro.

After that it seemed to go pretty well, at least at the start.

I got Stallone to tell the story of how he created Rocky and then to take us through his Hollywood career. He was open and honest about his rivalry with Arnold Schwarzenegger, his failures with the likes of *Stop Or My Mom Will Shoot* and his future plans with the Rocky spin-off franchise, *Creed*.

But then the effects of the booze began to kick in with some of the overly excited fans at the front—a couple of whom made drunken attempts to climb onto the stage shouting that they wanted to see if Rocky could really take a punch.

Acting as both security guard and host, I tried to discreetly shoo—and kick—their clambering fingers off the raised stage and carry on with the show as a suddenly weary looking Stallone made it clear I was on my own with this challenge. There was no sign of the Marines still being around to help us out of this tight spot. Time to make a sharp exit.

So, before a stage invasion by drunken brawlers could happen, I brought a swift end to the show, "Ladies and gentleman, what a night, please give it up for Sylvester Stallone!"

Long before the applause died down, and moments before the boozy mob made it up onto the platform, Sly and I were scurrying off to the sanctuary of backstage.

It was those next few minutes relaxing with him afterward, much more so than the hour and half interviewing him on stage, that were the true highlight of the evening for me. Because in that more relaxed atmosphere, I found my hero was all that I hoped he would be—really nice, chatty, and surprisingly down to earth.

WILLIAM SHATNER

Some say the greatest actor of all time is Laurence Olivier, others make the case for Robert De Niro, Meryl Streep, and more. But for me, the best of the best was and is William Shatner. Don't laugh.

I loved him as James T Kirk in *Star Trek* and later as Denny Crane in *Boston Legal* and the Shat was gloriously watchable in many other roles too.

But I had never met him and as he moved toward his eighties I was beginning to worry I'd missed my chance. And then I saw it while leafing through a magazine … a talk Shatner was to be giving in an L.A. hotel, "My Trek Through Acting."

I booked my ticket immediately and impatiently counted the days until the big show came around.

When it eventually did and I took my seat in the crowd, the first clue I got that this maybe wouldn't be the most conventional evening came when I saw the rest of the audience.

While I was dressed in a suit, they were dressed as Klingons. Not all of them, of course. There were also a few Ferengi, Vulcans, and a Romulan. But each to their own, every celebrity has a particular fan base, I suppose.

Kirk was always good with his stardates, so was Shatner. The great man appeared right on time. Though the doors opened with a creak rather than the swish of the Enterprise bridge.

He started off talking to us about some of the films he'd acted in. But instead of mentioning the classics, such as *Star Trek 2*, *Airplane 2,* and *Miss Congeniality 2*, he mentioned the lesser known films such as *Incubus*, *Kingdom of the Spiders,* and *Big Bad Mama.*

Shatner explained, "These rare films are not available in the shops but you can buy them from my website, williamshatner.com." Interesting to know.

He quickly moved on to talking about his recording career. Shatner has released several albums which, to put it kindly, have not exactly been critical favorites. He explained that many of them were not available in the shops—there's a surprise—but they were all available via WilliamShatner.com. No surprise.

Next it was plugs for the *Star Trek* novels he has written such as *Captain's Glory, Captain's Blood, Captain's Peril*—I've read them all.

Shatner said, "These books ARE available in the shops. For around ten dollars. But tonight you can buy any of them for a special price ... of twenty dollars."

Now I'm no economics expert but that seemed like something of a mark up to me. The big explanation was coming.

He took out a large gym bag and emptied the contents onto the table in front of him, a bunch of those *Star Trek* novels spilled out and he started arranging them before pulling out a sharpie pen and then cleared his throat.

"I'll autograph these books for twenty dollars and take pictures with each of you for thirty. Form an orderly line."

Well, the Klingons were on their feet in a second, the Vulcans too. But I was rooted to the spot.

The talk had lasted less than ten minutes and the rest of the hour was to be filled with a paid for signing session. Was my hero such a money grabber? How could that be when he reportedly made $80 million from his Priceline commercials and shares?

But this was the reality I was now facing. Still, not one to miss an opportunity I set about deciding what souvenir I should take from the evening.

I had all the Kirk books already but quite wanted a photo. However, having paid for my ticket to the (all too brief) talk I resented the idea of paying for a photo too. So I improvised.

7

Pulling out my camera, I walked to the side of the autograph line and tried to get a picture of Shatner as he signed books.

Well, there's clearly nothing wrong with his peripheral vision because the Shat spotted me trying to sneak a photo without paying and instantly covered his face with his hand to block my angle.

So I shifted position to try and get a better view when Shatner dropped four of the fingers in his hand and left the middle one pointing straight up.

When you get "flipped the bird" by your favorite TV star it's a disappointing situation. Even if I was asking for it.

I wish I had the picture but I was too disappointed in that moment to even click the shutter button. I beamed out of there as fast as possible.

Some years later, I interviewed Shatner for a business magazine and warily asked his advice about how people over the age of 65 could use their skills to reenter the workforce.

Happily, he didn't say by charging for their autograph at personal appearances. Instead he offered really good advice, such as lecturing, writing, retraining, and adapting, and couldn't have been nicer. Maybe I just got him on a bad day before.

In my eyes, Captain Kirk had redeemed himself and saved the day once more.

BRITNEY SPEARS

Many people meet the love of their life through work.

That's what I told myself when I was trying to pluck up the courage to ask Britney Spears out on a date.

It was twenty years ago when we were both a whole lot younger and she was in London to perform new single *Oops!... I Did It Again* on TV's *The Pepsi Chart Show*.

I was on assignment to spend a few hours watching the princess of pop rehearse and perform her latest hit.

It was very impressive, great dancing, great positivity, and professionalism and that tight red catsuit certainly had its charms.

There's been lots of talk about Brit using lip-synch to mime at concerts over the years but she did live vocals that night and was pitch perfect.

When we caught up after the show, I told her what a great experience it had been watching her work and how pleasing it was to see how she had treated everyone on the set so warmly. She seemed to like that and enjoyed our brief interview.

Encouraged, I mentioned that how being a long way from home she might like someone to show her the sights of London and I boldly offered my tour guide services.

"You mean, like a date?" she giggled.

"Er, well, not to put too fine a point on it, Britney, I suppose one could, in the light of day, see it like that, and, um, well, what I'm trying to say, one presumes, is, er, yes."

Suddenly she had me babbling like a Hugh Grant character!

Britney Spears threw her head back and laughed, "You're funny."

Then she was beckoned away by her manager and I never saw her again.

I like to imagine an alternative timeline in which Britney and I made it work and the world never learned the name Kevin Federline.

Ah, what might have been.

MORRISSEY

If there's one thing guaranteed to make me happy, it's listening to the miserable songs of my favorite pop star, Morrissey.

I don't know why, but those mournful lyrics about death and desperation combined with his deadpan style of delivery never fail to put a smile on my face.

I'm such a fan of the pope of mope's music that whenever I'm in his hometown of Manchester, I make a point of visiting a location associated with the man, be it Salford Lads Club, the cemetery gates he sang about when with The Smiths, or his surprisingly pleasant childhood home. Around the corner from that house is another regular haunt, the iron bridge referenced in one of the great Smiths songs, *Still Ill*, which fans from around the world have daubed with graffiti declaring their adoration of Morrissey.

Although I've seen Moz in concert more than any other artist and seem to bump into every celebrity eventually, I never expected to actually meet him as he's famously a reclusive enigma and not one for socializing.

So imagine my surprise when I encountered the monarch of misery at, of all places, a comedy show.

I was packed into a ninety-nine-seat Hollywood theatre to watch Russell Brand try out material for his upcoming stand-up comedy tour and the place was full apart from one plastic seat in front of mine with a paper 'reserved' sign taped to it written with a sharpie marker.

It appeared no one was going to sit there and I would have an unobstructed view of the show. But then the lights went down, Russell Brand took the stage and seconds later the occupant of the reserved seat walked in like a European prince and calmly took his seat. Morrissey! I could barely believe my eyes.

The show started and I couldn't tell you how good Russell's jokes were because I was only focused on the icon sitting directly in front.

It was remarkable to me how even in a relaxed, anonymous atmosphere like this he didn't once break character by being seen to smile.

While everyone else was laughing uproariously at the gags, I noticed Morrissey keeping up a running commentary saying, in a quiet voice, "that's a good one" or even "that's amusing." Perfect.

As the comedy continued, I turned my thoughts to what I could possibly say to my musical hero when the show ended and I would inevitably come face-to-face with him when he got up from his chair.

"Your music has meant so much to me," seemed so dull and predictable. Trying a joke seemed so risky. He didn't seem like the type to grant selfies. Maybe an old-fashioned autograph request might work. I knew I had a pen and paper at my feet in the Union Jack shoulder bag I carried everywhere.

While this last thought was in my head, I noticed the show was suddenly over, Russell Brand was taking his bows, and the audience was getting up to leave. I would have to be quick.

I raced up from my chair and in doing so accidentally kicked the bag at my feet, causing some of the contents, including my notepad and pen, to spill out at the feet of the star in front just as he turned around.

Morrissey looked at me and I looked at him. Then we both looked down at the shoulder bag. Morrissey looked back toward me and said, "I think you'll find that's your handbag."

I crouched down to scoop the contents back into the bag and as I did so, replied, "It's not a handbag!"

Then I rose to my full height of six feet two to confront Morrissey and bravely ask for my autograph … only to find he was gone. He vanished into the Hollywood night as if he was never there.

The only words I had managed to speak to the pop idol I so wanted to give my admiration to were, "It's not a handbag."

I've never seen him since. But I have been back to the iron bridge in Manchester. Amid all the chalk hearts, love declarations, and song lyrics graffitied on there I added my own cryptic words: "It's not a handbag."

I like to think that Morrissey fans have long puzzled over the meaning and origin of those words. Now they know.

SAMUEL L. JACKSON and GEORGE LUCAS

It's not every night you're at a urinal peeing in between two of your idols. But it does happen, at least if you're me.

I found myself flanked by *Star Wars* creator George Lucas and Hollywood acting great Samuel L. Jackson.

It was in the toilets of a London restaurant at the after-premiere party for a British film they were both associated with, *The 51st State*. When the famous duo appeared either side of me to answer the call of nature I didn't know where to look.

Maybe I should have just looked straight ahead rather than doing what I actually did.

First, I turned my head to the left and looked at Lucas with a dumb grin on my face which I hoped was conveying how much of a fan I was of his work but which I fear instead made me look vaguely stupid and creepy.

Then I turned right to smile at Jackson with that same slightly unhinged smile.

Only this time as I turned my head, I somehow turned my body too and ended up well, there's no elegant way to say this, peeing on Samuel L. Jackson's shoes.

Surveying the damage he delivered the one word that has become his fortune in so many films.

Quietly but forcefully before walking off to get cleaned up, he said, "Mother fucker!"

Thankfully, years later when I interviewed him in Hollywood, Sam didn't seem to remember me from the toilet incident.

We were having a great chat on stage in front of a packed audience who had just enjoyed a preview screening of his revisionist western set in the Antebellum South, *Django Unchained*. Our Q&A had covered everything from cowboys to slavery and writer–director Quentin Tarantino. All was going well until we went to questions from the audience.

The first couple were fine but then this little old lady at the front put her hand up and, not even waiting to be called, yelled out, "Why did there have to be so much bad language in it?"

Jackson asked her what language in particular had been so offensive and she replied, "I don't understand why everyone had to use the N-word so much."

Mocking confusion over what word she meant, Jackson theatrically said, "Nincompoop?"

Not getting it, the old lady got frustrated. "No, not that one."

He tried again. "Nobody?"

The audience of four hundred and fifty shifted uncomfortably in their seats at the awkward moment and then she let him have it, shouting out: "N----r!"

There was silence in the screening room.

Cool as you like, Samuel L. Jackson asked her, "Do you feel better now you've called me that?"

I almost pissed myself.

TOM CRUISE

The first time I met Tom Cruise, I headbutted him.

It was an accident I tell you, seriously, it was. There were crowds, excitement, I was still new in town, and I was possibly just a bit too enthusiastic.

Enthusiasm is a natural state for Tom who, on the handful of occasions I've seen him since, has always been very upbeat and smiley.

But I was hugely hyped up at that first chance to shake hands with a star who ever since his breakthrough hit *Top Gun* had seemed to me like an almost otherworldly being.

I've since come to know that despite all the fame and mystique, he's just like everyone else—except probably more polite and friendly.

But that first time we met I still remember the sound of my teeth clinking hard in my mouth when I was introduced to the megastar at a film premiere.

I also remember being surprised at how much shorter he seemed than in the movies. I thought, "Wow, he really must be a superb actor to convince the world he can beat up so many bad guys in action movies. In real life, he's so unassuming, and me being six foot two, I look like I could take him."

Snapping out of my thoughts, I managed to mumble, "Such a pleasure to meet you, Tom" as I leaned forward—and down—to shake his hand.

At the same time, smiley Tom was stepping forward—and up—and then … thwack!

My head connected with his nose and Cruise wheeled away in pain holding that $20 million face.

In the couple of seconds that followed, all manner of jumbled thoughts flooded my brain.

Had I hurt him? And what would the consequence be for me at injuring Hollywood's biggest star? I remember those crazy thoughts in this order ... "Given his power and fame he could maybe end my showbiz reporting career, get me kicked out of the country and sent back to England ... or even thrown in a Scientology jail."

Tom Cruise probably doesn't even remember this but in that moment he held the future of my life in his hands.

Luckily for me he couldn't have been nicer, laughed, and said, "Don't worry about it man."

Happily recovered, he shook the next waiting hand.

Thanks for being so good about it Tom.

ROBERT DE NIRO

Friends call him Bob. So I call him Mr. De Niro.

We've met a handful of times. He wouldn't remember.

But meeting the great actor has never been a great experience.

I've heard he's shy and socially awkward, or maybe he's got no time for the likes of me.

The more engaging and polite I've tried to be, the more disinterested he always seems.

Maybe it's cultural differences. New Yorkers like him are supposed to be brash types who look at Englishmen like me as timid tea drinkers. But I've never subscribed to stereotypes, and certainly not in the case of him or me. I just wish we could find a better connection.

Robert De Niro is electrifying on screen but dull in real life, at least with me.

One of our more exasperating encounters came in Dubai at a summit of world leaders and influencers.

He was there to talk about climate change, presumably from an expert perspective.

But he seemed to know, or recall, disappointingly little about the topic.

Whenever I fired a question at him that required specifics, he would confer with the woman standing at his shoulder, presumably a true expert, and repeat as his answer, parrot fashion, exactly what she had told him.

Whether I asked about hurricanes, floods, droughts, or other natural disasters and how best to prepare for them, it was the same pattern each time, conferring with the expert before answering.

As the bizarre exchange continued, it took all my professionalism not to quote his famous line from *TaxiDriver* and ask De Niro, "Are you talking to me?" It seemed that day he did most of his talking to her.

AL PACINO

You have never truly been in the presence of greatness until Al Pacino has spat on you.

It happened to me at L.A.'s Wadsworth Theatre where Al was giving it all in one of his shouty but mesmerizing performances.

I was fortunate enough to get a front row seat to a performance of the Oscar Wilde play *Salome* in which Pacino was playing King Herod in the story of the biblical bad guy's obsession with his beautiful stepdaughter, played by Jessica Chastain.

So committed was Al that he was spitting while delivering many lines—and it was landing on the front row.

Whenever he stepped to the edge of the stage, his spittle always seemed to project to the right—so eventually I would lean left ensuring the couple sitting to the right of me took most of it.

A year or so later, I got to meet Al when he had made a film about *Salome*, produced by my friend Barry Navidi who recommended me as the onstage interviewer when Pacino set about promoting the movie to audiences.

We got along well from the start—and he didn't spit on me once.

Al seemed especially pleased that I'd seen and could discuss the three little seen films which mean the most to him, passion projects *The Local Stigmatic, Chinese Coffee,* and *Looking For Richard.* While everyone wants to talk to him about *The Godfather* and *Scarface,* it's the smaller movies which he somehow seems to care about more than the blockbusters.

I've interviewed Al several times since and each time have learned some obscure but intriguing detail I never knew before, whether it's the history of traveling minstrels in acting or the preparation rituals of long forgotten stage performers. That's because he's a walking, talking encyclopedia of acting history, who seems to know every play ever written.

At eighty, he's still at the top of his game and a revered movie star. But it seems to me from spending time with him that Al Pacino would be happiest running a ninety-nine-seat theater producing experimental plays.

MADONNA

I've noticed that the mark of a star is how long they keep the press waiting for an interview.

Madonna proved herself a true megastar by being three hours late for the UK press call for her *Evita* movie.

I didn't care—I was such a fan that I would have waited three hundred hours for the Material Girl to make her entrance.

As she eventually strolled into a London hotel ballroom and took her place on the raised stage between *Evita* costars Antonio Banderas and Jimmy Nail, my notebook was open but so was my mouth. I'd met royalty, legends, and all manner of icons yet this was the only time I had ever been starstruck.

It was an unfamiliar, woozy, feeling for me, like the room was spinning and my heart beating at express speed. Understandable though. I knew every lyric of the *True Blue* album by heart, I'd had the record poster on my wall and now, ten years later, she was just ten feet in front of my seat at her press conference.

The next few minutes were something of a daze. I somehow pulled myself together enough to switch on my tape recorder to capture the quotes but couldn't make notes or even focus on what was being said.

Before I knew it, the moderator was saying, "just five minutes left for questions." I had to take my chance to speak to her now. But what would I say to the Queen of Pop?

My hand went straight up and when I was called upon I somehow found myself saying the following words … "Madonna, the whole nation is behind you and pulling for the success of this film. On behalf of the people of Britain, may I approach the stage and give you a symbolic good luck kiss?"

To my surprise, she extended one arm, like she was the Pope or something, and said, "You may kiss my hand."

Well I didn't need a second invitation so I sprang from my seat.

I kissed Madonna's hand—ice cold—and couldn't believe my luck at an ambition achieved. I just stood there smiling and saying, "Thank you. Thank you."

Moments later I was lifted off my feet by her six foot ten security guard who expertly flung me back in my front row seat before my feet even touched the ground. I guess he thought I'd got too close to the boss and wasn't retreating fast enough.

But, hey, I had kissed Madonna! My feet still haven't touched the ground.

BUZZ ALDRIN

When I went to interview the second man on the Moon, I thought it wise not to ask how he felt about rumors that the moon landing had been faked in a Hollywood film studio.

The last man to ask that, Bart Sibrel, had ended up punched firmly in the face by the space hero who had been developing quite a reputation for getting rough in response to such questions.

But it turned out Buzz had plenty more interesting stuff to say in an out-of-this-world interview.

He told me setting foot on the Moon wasn't the only great achievement of his life—as beating alcoholism and depression scored highly too.

In a remarkably frank chat, the man who made his name reaching for the stars confessed he'd spent many of the years afterward reaching for the bottle.

When he came back down to earth he didn't know what to do with the rest of his life, hadn't got rich as endorsement deals didn't really exist then, became depressed, started drinking, wrecked his first and second marriages, and ended up selling cars for a living—when he wasn't drunkenly wrecking them in crashes.

Therapy had since helped him conquer his demons and lucrative talks on the guest speaker circuit propped up his bank account.

Now he runs a foundation encouraging the further exploration of space and sharing the wonders of the galaxy with children.

I was so inspired by his parting words to me. "I am still awed by the miracle of having walked on the Moon. That awe in each of us must be the engine of future achievement, not a slow dimming light from a time once bright."

Now let's switch from the moon and get back to more stars....

ELTON JOHN

I could barely believe my luck when I found myself seated on the next table to Elton John at top Los Angeles restaurant, *Craig's*. Surely the moment had come to finally meet one of my heroes who I'd only previously seen from audience seats at his concerts.

Looking at the two bodyguards standing either side of the table the pop icon was sharing with husband David Furnish and Hollywood executive Jeffrey Katzenberg, it seemed Elton didn't want to be disturbed.

I was just working out my tactics for approaching him when the silence was shattered by cries of ' Elton! Elton!' coming from across the restaurant.

I turned around to see a man with long-ish grey hair who had just walked in and was bounding toward Elton's table yelling, "It's me, Jon! It's Jon! "

As the bodyguards shifted uncomfortably wondering whether this interloper was dangerous, and so did I, it wasn't hard to notice Elton looking uncomfortable too. Until … the shouty guy added, 'Bon Jovi! Jon Bon Jovi! '

Wow, he sure looks different now than in the *Livin' on a Prayer* video.

Jon Bon Jovi eagerly took the spare seat at the table offered by Elton and that was the end of my chance of grabbing it.

I did eventually get to meet Elton on the awards circuit during the success of his superb biopic, *Rocketman,* and he was lovely. So too was his husband David Furnish.

But I hit it off best of all with Elton's lyricist Bernie Taupin, another great talent and fascinating person—who it turns out is as good an artist as he is a songwriter—and I'm now so proud to now call him a friend.

The world's most creative talents have held a lifelong fascination for me and it's a remarkable thing to not only meet and interview them but in some cases befriend them too.

CLINT EASTWOOD

It could be argued that I owe my career to Clint Eastwood.

To get into my dream journalism school, the University of Central Lancashire, I needed good exam results from college and while English was not a problem, I was struggling in politics.

Researching small-town American politics was proving a particular problem—until I hit on a wild idea.

Movie star Clint Eastwood had been elected mayor of the small but stylish seaside town of Carmel in his home state of California a couple of years earlier so I wrote to him at Carmel City Hall asking for help with my politics project.

Imagine my surprise two weeks later when a large air mail envelope dropped through my letterbox containing a bunch of Clint's election campaign literature, manifesto, leaflets, press releases, and some documents of office together with a sweet personal note.

I used all that stuff as the basis for my pass grade in politics which helped me get into journalism school and the rest, as they say, is history.

Years later I was able to meet the screen legend in Hollywood and thank him—but it didn't go as smoothly as I'd like because I got very excited and ended up tripping over my words so must have sounded like a gibbering idiot.

But I've since gotten to know his lovely and multitalented daughter Alison Eastwood and explained how much her dad's kindness meant to me.

One Sunday morning late in 2019, I got a very disturbing call from a producer at BBC News asking me to check out an internet rumor that Clint Eastwood had died and if it was true could I go on air and pay tribute.

I'm sure there are staff at the Beeb who think of me as the Angel of Death because they always seem to call me when a star dies as I apparently am good at striking the right tone for such somber occasions.

But one thing I've learned from experience with such things is to make sure the person in question is actually dead.

In these situations, my mind always flashes back to the day one of my bosses on a British tabloid had assured me that actor Brian Croucher, best known for UK sci-fi series *Blake's 7,* had died that morning. My boss sent me round to his home in Surrey to get an interview with the grieving widow.

Mrs. Croucher seemed very confused when I knocked on the door saying how sorry I was for her loss—especially as her husband was alive and well and sitting in the kitchen!

I made my apologies and left—but not before the couple had very kindly offered me tea and biscuits.

It was from that moment on that I resolved never to believe a rumor of a celebrity death until I had personally checked it out and satisfied myself this was safe to report.

So I had to make a very uncomfortable call to Alison Eastwood, and her artist husband Stacy, aware that there were disturbing rumors about Clint's health on the internet and I hoped they understood the need to check such things out in a sensitive manner before rushing to report them as anything close to facts.

Luckily, they must have seen the funny side because the message came back that such rumors seem to circulate all the time and Clint was perfectly fine.

When I next see him, I want to ask why he never chose to go further in politics than the local level. Imagine how cool it would be to have President Eastwood.

STEVIE WONDER

I've never wanted to be famous myself. I just can't see the appeal of having strangers coming up all the time and making you feel like public property.

Especially now in the selfie era where so many people demand photos. But some of them don't even ask.

The worst example of this came when I saw what happened to Stevie Wonder.

I was attending a charity foundation dinner and performance where he was to sing but before that we were all at long tables enjoying our salads.

To my horror, I saw countless attendees leaving their seats to creep up behind the singer while he was eating and pose for selfies with him as if he was a wax figure rather than a real person.

It was as if they thought just because he was blind he somehow couldn't sense them hovering beside him with their camera phones out.

Just as I was about to loudly protest their behavior, there was a sudden commotion caused by another famous guest.

Smokey Robinson was walking out in a huff after a waiter spilled wine all over his pink jacket.

And the Stevie Wonder 'fans' wandered off to try and get pictures with him instead before Smokey bolted for the exit.

But dignified Stevie never complained in the face of the terrible treatment he received from some guests at that charity dinner.

Minutes later he was up on stage performing for them and the rest of us and reminding everyone of the brilliant talent that makes him such a class act.

PRISCILLA PRESLEY

The first time I met Priscilla Presley it seemed wise not to mention I was banned from Graceland.

That had been where she'd lived with Elvis and shared one of America's most epic love stories until leaving the marriage being unable to stop his downward spiral.

But, from talking to her, I got the sense she had never stopped loving him and maybe that's why she opened the Memphis mansion to the public and built it into one of the country's most popular tourist attractions.

It was as a tourist that I had visited Graceland and rather foolishly wandered away from the official tour group into the roped off no-go area of the ground floor bathroom.

That's where Elvis had died, reportedly sitting on the toilet, straining hard to have a bowel movement, suffering a heart attack and keeling over onto the floor.

And I'm not proud of this but I was curious to see the place where The King spent his final moments.

To me that bathroom at Graceland has as much historical significance as the Pyramids at Giza, The Parthenon, or the Taj Mahal.

After creeping away from the group and carefully stepping over the velvet rope, security stepped in before I could even get my camera out, hauled me out of the building, and told me never to return.

I went back to where I was staying in Memphis, the Heartbreak Hotel, which—true story—was actually down at the end of Lonely Street, and reflected I would never get that close to Elvis again.

That assumption turned out to be wrong. I actually interviewed him from beyond the grave a few years later.

Using the services of a medium at a séance, I fired questions via her to Elvis, demanding to know how he rated the talents of the biggest pop star of that time, Justin Bieber.

Sadly, I never got my answer because all The King would say in response via the medium, and in that trademark drawl, was, "I'm hungry. I'm so hungry." What a shame. I guess they don't have enough peanut butter and banana sandwiches up in heaven to keep him happy.

This was another story I didn't tell to Priscilla when I found myself sitting next to her at a dinner party for influencers and influential people.

Instead we found ourselves talking about personal security because the dinner guest opposite us was the then chief of police in Los Angeles, Charlie Beck.

Priscilla, who seems a quiet, lovely, diffident person, tentatively asked him if it was legal for someone who worried about their own safety to keep a gun in the glove box of their car.

Chief Beck, who was charming but firm, replied, "Do I have to send one of my officers out to the valet parking stand to check your car for weapons?"

Nervous, Priscilla stammered, "Er, what, no. Just asking for a friend."

Beck calmly explained it was important not to keep a gun at all unless you were an expert in how to use it. He said it would be more likely to hurt you and your loved ones than any intruder.

Chastened by her lesson in gun control from the top cop, Priscilla seemed relaxed to talk to me instead about all she was doing to further develop the tourist experience at Graceland.

In the hope they've forgotten about me there by now, maybe I'll risk a return visit. I promise I'll be wise and respectful enough next time to stay out of Elvis's bathroom.

PAUL McCARTNEY

I was such an idiot when I interviewed the great Paul McCartney.

Driving to Liverpool for our chat, I knew I'd be starstruck in his presence but was determined not to come across like Chris Farley in that famous *Saturday Night Live* sketch where he played an interviewer so overwhelmed to meet a member of The Beatles that he could ask nothing but dumb, fawning questions.

I wanted Paul to be impressed by me and, as a result, tried too hard to act like some great interviewer rather than just asking sensible questions like I would of anyone else.

This was at the opening of LIPA, or Liverpool Institute of the Performing Arts, a new *Fame* style academy on the old site of his closed boyhood school.

Macca wanted to make the long and winding road to stardom a little easier for the next generation of talented youngsters and had pumped a million pounds of his own money into the project. Plus he was going to be teaching songwriting as part of the curriculum.

For the first time ever, my questions had a cynical side to them. I would ask things like, "With all your money what do you really know about the struggles and dreams of today's youngsters in Liverpool?"

McCartney took it all in good grace and said that he and the other teachers hoped to nurture the talent by giving them inside knowledge about aspects of the industry these students maybe could not find elsewhere.

I guess he's seen it all in his career and nothing phases him at this point. I really liked him although I didn't much like myself that day.

It's been such a pleasure since to become close friends with Paul's step-mother and stepsister, Angie McCartney and Ruth McCartney, a fab duo who possess plenty of Beatles style magic of their own.

MERYL STREEP

I t's hard to imagine a star of the magnitude of Meryl Streep asking for anyone's autograph.

But even superstars have idols just like the rest of us.

In her case, as she confided in me, her hero was the composer Stephen Sondheim.

When she got to work on the movie version of one of his musicals, *Into the Woods*, Meryl took her chance to meet him.

She went up to the composer at the recording session of the film's soundtrack and asked Sondheim to sign her copy of the sheet of his music that she was about to sing.

He said he'd be delighted to do so and scrawled these unforgettable words next to his signature, "Don't f--- it up!"

Not many people use that kind of language with Meryl, which is perhaps why she was so delighted to tell the story.

It was interesting meeting the living legend of acting. She was approachable, funny, and a little clumsy.

I've encountered her a couple of times since and on each occasion she's either tripped or banged into something, which for someone who gives such faultless performances, is kind of endearing.

HUGH HEFNER

I've been to Buckingham Palace, the White House, and many other iconic buildings of the world. But there's nowhere that beats the Playboy Mansion.

The history, the headlines, and the sexiness of the place make it so special and so when I got an invite to go there and interview *Playboy* founder Hugh Hefner, I felt like a dog with two, er, bones.

As I drove up to the gates, there didn't seem any bells or buzzers to alert Hef to my arrival. But suddenly I heard a disembodied voice saying, "Good morning."

Looking around in confusion for where the sound was coming from, I heard, "Is that Sandro?" coming from a large rock on the ground.

"Um, er, yes," I replied, speaking directly into the rock, which turned out to house a hidden intercom system.

The voice said to me, "When the gates open, drive to the top of the path, park there, and you'll be greeted by your personal bunny, Lauren."

Personal bunny???

I must have driven up that long, winding path at a hundred miles an hour.

Sure enough when I parked, Lauren was waiting for me, dressed in the iconic bunny girl outfit. Nice tail.

Linking my arm, the beautiful guide said, "Let me first give you a tour of the private zoo."

She could have given me a tour of a cardboard box and I would have loved every second of it.

As Lauren showed me a pair of chimpanzees and I asked if they ever got up to any monkey business, the bunny ignored my pathetic attempt at humor and regaled me with the history of the building.

I knew it already from countless books, documentaries, and movies but every word from her lips was like poetry to me so I didn't mind.

We next strolled over to the famous grotto, scene of so many debauched gatherings down the years. I half expected to find James Caan in there still hanging around from some swinging seventies party but it was empty and placid that sunny March morning.

Then it was time to take me into the main house to met Hef and moments later there he was in the doorway, complete with trademark robe. I couldn't believe I was finally meeting him: the Walt Disney of adult entertainment.

Lauren left us, sadly never to reappear, and the interview began.

Hef talked me through some of the highlights of his life, telling how Marilyn Monroe was the first cover girl on the launch issue of *Playboy* magazine in 1953, and how he had donated money to save the iconic Hollywood sign and owned the letter Y of that long-standing landmark.

He added that he still picked the centerfolds for every issue of his magazine but I got the impression he didn't seem as involved with it as he had once been and the more we talked the more I felt he seemed a little cut off from his empire.

Anyway it must have gone well because Hefner invited me to join him and his girlfriends—plural—at a club that night.

I did so and Hef and his three blonde girlfriends sat in a roped off VIP area enjoying table service and the finest champagne but he soon fell asleep and the girlfriends just spoke to each other. I wasn't allowed to speak to them and that may not have just been a rule for press because it appeared they were encouraged to speak to Hef and no other men.

So I slipped away with my last image of Hefner asleep on the shoulder of a buxom blonde.

He died in 2017, aged 91, but I've visited his grave at least once a year since. It's the plot right next to Marilyn Monroe in the Westwood Village Memorial Park Cemetery.

As he had said before, and repeated in our interview when I asked Hef why he'd bought the $75,000 crypt years earlier, "Spending eternity next to Marilyn is an opportunity too sweet to pass up."

PRINCESS DIANA

When I was first approached to be a royal reporter, I recoiled at the idea.

"But-but-but" I protested to my paper's news editor, "I can't be around those people because I don't believe it's right in this day and age to bow and scrape to other human beings."

He nodded as if that was a fair point and asked me what else I thought about the royals.

I said, "The Queen should clear off to Windsor Castle, move out of Buckingham Palace, and turn that place into a shelter for the London homeless. With all those rooms it would be a great help to the problem and a popular gesture with the public."

He said that was exactly the questioning attitude needed in royal reporting, rather than the "tugging the forelock" approach taken by other royal correspondents. I was hired.

I still suspected I was only getting the job because I was the youngest reporter in the office and, therefore, least likely to protest vigorously.

Other journalists told me it was a terrible gig because unlike in other fields, the protocol with the royals is you can't ask them a question until they have spoken to you first. They said it was an easier beat for photographers than for those who rely on the written and spoken word.

So it was with a certain amount of reluctance that I set off on the royal circuit. But with a certain enthusiasm too as the main figure I would be reporting on would be Princess Diana, who was pretty much the biggest star on the planet.

Looking at her story as an outsider, especially her split from Charles, independent streak and support of causes outside royal norms, I thought Diana was great—something of a rebel against an archaic institution and that side of her fascinated me.

But we didn't get off to the best start.

She took exception to a front-page story of mine headlined, "My boobs are too small, moans Di."

Even though Diana had said it to a few people within my earshot, she wasn't amused that I had reported the quote.

But as I became more of a regular fixture at her public appearances and press events, the attitude softened, I got the occasional smile and my admiration for her grew. In a few ways … Diana was very aware of her public image and became increasingly adept at how to steer things in her favor with a carefully chosen look, photo op, or well-timed remark or appearance and, contrary to popular belief, the press loved her.

There was a genuine caring nature within her and an interest in other people which couldn't be faked and came out in all those events and visits I covered. But most of all, there was a deep love for her sons and a determination to give them as normal of an upbringing as possible given their extraordinary circumstances.

As we know, her life was cut short in such a sudden and tragic way.

On that terrible day, August 31, 1997, I was as devastated and dazed as the rest of the world and felt the loss like it was one of my own relatives.

Having started to mix showbiz reporting with royal coverage by then, I was on a week off from the paper filming a TV celebrity interview series at the time that the dreadful news came through from Paris. The circumstances seemed as unreal as many a Hollywood movie and much more sad.

With Diana gone, I felt I couldn't go back to royal reporting but switched to showbiz full time instead.

It was many years later when I went back to it, covering royalty for CNN International and Headline News around the time that Meghan

Markle appeared on the scene. There's another big personality who divides opinion but always makes for a good story.

Being drawn back into the royal world so many years later, and covering Diana's now grown sons, made me reassess the royal family as an institution. I see more good in it than I did before.

Maybe it's part of getting older, maybe it's to do with not living in Britain anymore—it's often said there's nothing more patriotic than a Brit who no longer lives there—but the support the royals give for charities and their symbolism for the nation are things I feel more positively about now.

So much so that I'm on the board of trustees for the Royal Society of St George, the Queen's charity in America, which exists to slay metaphorical dragons by helping causes close to the heart and values of the palace.

It's a dramatic change from where I was. But I have Princess Diana to thank for making me see things differently.

PRINCE CHARLES

We are used to seeing royalty at film premieres in London, but it's a most unusual thing in Los Angeles where the protocol of how to greet the royals is a mystery to many.

I certainly found that out while covering the first Hollywood movie premiere attended by Prince Charles—the launch of his friend Kenneth Branagh's *Frankenstein* film in the mid-nineties.

The normal rules didn't seem to apply to Charles either. Like many of the stars on the red carpet outside the Cineplex Odeon that night, he was signing autographs for the clamoring fans—you wouldn't get that back home.

Charles had always seemed very stiff and formal in the UK—a lifetime training for the throne will do that to you—but in L.A. he appeared unusually relaxed.

After the screening, I saw Danny DeVito throwing an arm around the prince, who promised to look him up next time he was in Tinseltown.

Then Kramer from Seinfeld, Michael Richards, was trying to explain to the royal guest who he was—a tricky task as I knew Charles didn't spend much time watching American sitcoms, and barely watched TV at all.

Next we all headed off to the after-party in the ballroom of the Century Plaza Hotel across the street and after the initial excitement of sharing the room with a royal, the place soon thinned out as Hollywood executives remembered they had to be up early for pilates and power meetings.

Among the few left were Kenneth Branagh and a bemused Prince Charles who I heard telling the star of the film that he was "not used to this as in Britain no one leaves before I do."

Hollywood isn't Britain, your Royal Highness. We do things differently here.

DONALD TRUMP

Every time I visit New York, there's one magical place I always visit on Fifth Avenue—Tiffany's.

That's because *Breakfast at Tiffany's* is my favorite movie and I never tire of standing where Audrey Hepburn stood in that beautiful film.

Another part of my NYC routine is to visit Trump Tower right after Tiffany's. The shopping and residential complex is next door and the food court or bar there has long been a welcome place to sit down as a break from the slog of walking through the packed Manhattan streets.

In the years before Trump became President, this building had come to international prominence as the main setting of his hit TV series, *The Apprentice*.

On a visit there in 2012, I was checking out gift items in the kiosk off the lobby of Trump Tower and after seeing ties and books noticed a new cologne for men Trump had brought out, amusingly called Success.

"Does this have a sweet smell?" I asked the salesman behind the counter, who, not getting my attempted joke, replied, "Yes, it's a fresh and woodsy scent thanks to being a blend of juniper, birch wood, and ginger. Why don't you try it?"

He indicated a sample bottle on the counter and as I picked it up to spray myself on the neck, I was suddenly startled to see the man himself, Donald Trump, emerging from the elevator and walking past me toward the street. While distracted, I accidentally sprayed myself not on the wrist as intended but in the eyes.

Temporarily blinded by the spray and also staggering back from the slightly overpowering smell, I came to a halt right in front of Donald Trump, wiping my eyes still with the tester bottle in my hand.

Ever the salesman, Trump said, "That cologne is fantastic. It's the best," and then turned and went about his day.

Well, he's not that good a salesman. I didn't buy a bottle of Success.

Talking of success, I never thought then that four years later Donald Trump would be elected President of the United States. To be fair, I still didn't think it four hours before he was declared the winner of the 2016 election.

I never talk about him on TV, as I prefer to stay out of politics these days, but I can't say I agree with a lot of his decisions from the White House.

However, there was one decision of his that I was very grateful for.

Framed on my wall next to a signed letter to me from President Trump sent "on behalf of a grateful Nation," is a medal, The President's Volunteer Service Award, given to me in recognition of community and charity work I've done for the betterment of others.

I've never worn the "Trump medal" in public because it's so gigantic and bombastic it looks like something only rapper Flavor Flav could carry off with confidence.

LIZA MINNELLI

Liza Minnelli once threw a black pudding at me.

The star was on a visit to northern England so I decided to welcome her to the area by presenting the star with the local delicacy.

But the welcome gesture backfired as she recoiled from horror like the dish was radioactive and threw it back in my face.

I explained that it was merely a blood sausage made from pork blood—but that didn't seem to help matters and her security team moved in and swiftly cancelled our scheduled interview.

My life is a cabaret old chum.

CHAPTER 2:

SANDRO AND THE STARS

BARRY MANILOW

Maybe you were lucky enough to grow up in a household where you were exposed to great music like The Beatles, David Bowie, or The Rolling Stones. Not me.

The soundtrack of my childhood was Barry Manilow.

My mother loved his hits like *Mandy*, *Copacabana*, and *I Write the Songs* and so I grew up exposed to them, like it or not. He was her favorite and mum's passion for Barry continued for years even though she'd never seen him perform live.

So when I was looking for a special sixtieth birthday present for her, I arranged to fly my mum to Las Vegas where the cheesy, if only to me, singer was in residency and got tickets to take her to the show.

I'd found during research that there was a bit in each concert where Barry brings a member of the audience up on stage and sings *Can't Smile Without You* to them. Upon arrival at the showroom I gave a big tip to the usher showing us to our seats and stressed how much my mother would like to be called up on stage.

So the concert began and it was brilliant watching mum's joyous face as Bazza rattled through the hits. I still didn't like the songs that make the whole world sick, er, I mean sing—but I loved that she was so happy.

Then it happened. The band struck up the first few notes of *Can't Smile Without You* and Barry asked the crowd if there was anyone in the audience who wanted to come on stage so he could sing to them. Well, almost every hand in the place shot up. My mum put both hands in the air. And she shouted, "Me, Barry!"

The headliner really milked the moment like a classic showbiz ham. Walking to the left of the stage and gazing out, then walking to the right trying to spot just the right audience member before Barry stopped center stage, gazed out to just where my mother was out of her chair pleading, pointed in her direction and said, "I see a lovely lady there. You! Come on down."

Well, despite her bad hip, my mum vaulted from her chair and raced to the stage like an overly enthusiastic contestant on *The Price is Right*, shouting as she ran, "I'm coming, Barry."

I was almost as excited as she was and could feel her excitement as she rushed to the stage.

Mum got right to the edge of the stage and then Manilow looked down at her, screwed up his face, and delivered seven devastating words.

"Not you. The pretty woman behind you."

I couldn't believe it either.

My beautiful mum turned away disappointed as the far less pretty woman took the stage with a seemingly oblivious Barry who launched into *Can't Smile Without You.*

At that moment, I wondered if my mother would ever smile again. She trudged back to me and quietly asked, "Can we go?" We left. Silently.

Mum can laugh about it all now. But she has never listened to Manilow again. I don't blame her if that's typical of the way he speaks to his fans.

BRAD PITT

Imagine getting this assignment from your boss: "Find Brad Pitt, sniff him, and find out if it's true that he smells."

Well, I did all three—and certainly got the answer.

But something really stank about that task, which I was given back in my London newspaper days.

My editor told me there was a rumor going around that the world's sexiest man, Brad Pitt, suffered terribly from body odor—supposedly by not showering after his morning trip to the gym.

There was also a tip that the Hollywood star had a lunch reservation at a central London restaurant that day so I was told to head down there and bring back the story.

Reluctantly, off I went. I took a seat at the bar, scanned the restaurant, and, sure enough, there was Brad at the very back dining with some agent looking type.

Now I had to work out how to proceed. Maybe I should just walk up and sniff him. So I set off toward his table.

I was just approaching where Brad and his guest were sitting when the head waiter blocked my path and said, in a rather snooty tone, "Can I help you with something, sir?" Think fast, Sandro!

"Yes, I was just looking for the gents' toilet."

He pointed it out and in I went.

Hanging around in a cubicle of the gents, I worked out a plan. Chances had to be good that if I stayed in there long enough Brad would eventually visit the loo.

That way I could discreetly check out if he ponged and what his bathroom hygiene routine was—maybe he wouldn't wash his hands.

Ten minutes later, as I now lingered by the sinks, Brad still hadn't appeared and I could tell the bathroom attendant was wondering why one of his customers was staying in here so long.

To avoid any awkward questions, I put a crisp five pound note in his tip tray, smiled, and carried on waiting. I started to wash and dry my hands. Then I sprayed on some of the expensive looking cologne that was on the basin.

Happily, just a moment later, Brad Pitt breezed into the bathroom, walked straight into the cubicle I'd just exited and I took up a position by the central sink then waited for my target, feeling like an assassin from a spy movie.

Brad Pitt emerged shortly afterward, stood beside me at the sinks, gazed into the mirror and then I took my chance—I leaned over and sniffed him. I couldn't smell anything unpleasant, so I leaned in a bit nearer.

Suddenly Brad turned toward me, a puzzled look on his face, and asked, "Can I help you, buddy?"

Think fast once more, Sandro.

"Er yes, I was wondering if you wanted to try any of these after shaves."

Brad said, "No, thank you" and, clearly feeling a bit awkward, turned to leave—without washing his hands!

Then the bathroom attendant appeared from nowhere holding a toilet roll and said, in an accent I couldn't place, "Autograph. Now. Please."

Brad, looking very confused now, was just explaining that he didn't have a pen when some panic and madness took me over and for some reason I decided to spray the star with the same cologne I had just used.

But he turned away at that moment and instead of spraying him on the neck I managed to get him right between the eyes. This was a foreshadowing of the Donald Trump fragrance incident I mentioned in the previous chapter.

Temporarily blinded, Pitt spiraled around the bathroom, then out of the door and back to his lunch guest.

Thinking it best, I stayed in the gents until Brad had left the restaurant.

Then I went back to the office ready to tell my boss that while Brad didn't smell, he didn't wash his hands in the bathroom.

But luckily he wasn't interested because a proper news story was breaking and he needed all reporters to focus on that one immediately.

I can't for the life of me remember what the other story was, but I'm so glad I have now moved on in my career than I can interview Brad Pitt like a normal person rather than having to ambush him in toilets.

REESE WITHERSPOON

I'd gone to my local movie theatre for an afternoon screening of the comedy *Bridesmaids* but found it hard to concentrate on the film when I saw who was sitting across the aisle from me.

There, in baggy workout clothes and sitting with a couple of friends, was Reese Witherspoon, who was enjoying a snack.

And when I say enjoying, I mean really enjoying….

She was chugging from a box of candy, full of chocolate malted milk balls.

It's just not the kind of sight you expect to see from health-conscious beautiful movie stars—although it made me really warm to her. Stars, they're just like us after all!

Anyway, if you've seen the movie you'll know the funniest moment comes in the bridal shop with the diarrhea scene.

Everyone in the audience was laughing at that part and Reese laughed so hysterically that her left arm went up in the air involuntarily and a bunch of chocolate malted milk balls arched out of the box, into the air, landed, and rolled across the floor, a couple landing at my feet.

Now most of us would have just left things there. Not Reese. She got down on her hands and knees and started picking them up, even crawling over to me and scooping up the last two.

I was terribly worried she was going to stick them in her mouth but happily she gathered them all up and threw them in the bin at the back of the room before returning to her seat.

Every time I see *Bridesmaids* now, I think of Reese Witherspoon down on all fours looking for her balls.

CHRISTIAN BALE

I was a bit nervous to meet Christian Bale as his tough guy reputation goes before him.

You've probably seen that YouTube clip of him screaming with foul-mouthed fury at a crew member on the set of *Terminator Salvation*.

And let's not forget he was released on police bail after the *Batman Begins* premiere having been questioned over an alleged assault on his own mother and sister.

If you're thinking this is a preamble to me saying he was as gentle as a lamb, well, you're wrong.

My tactic when Christian walked into the room where I was going to interview him was to fall back on the default position I always use with angry people: charm them with kindness.

So the second I saw him, I rushed up with my most beaming smile, saying, "Hi, thanks for being here, I'm Sandro and it's my great pleasure to be interviewing you today."

He roared back, "I'm on the bloody phone!"

I hadn't realized he had an earpiece in and was mid-conversation.

With him was his wife, Sibi, who introduced herself, apologized for her husband's abruptness, and explained he was talking to their landscape gardener.

I hovered around listening in to the call feeling very sorry for the gardener as Christian seemed very impatient about the petunias.

He ended the call, then thrust out his hand, and said, "Hi, I'm Christian."

I was fascinated by his speaking voice.

Knowing that he'd grown up in Wales but lived in Los Angeles most of his life I guess I expected him to sound like a cross between Richard Burton and a surfer dude.

Instead he sounded like, well, Batman.

Our interview was an unusual one because while he answered all the questions just fine, he didn't respond to any of my attempts at levity and seemed to have a total absence of a sense of humor.

I've loved most of his films, and think no one plays a brooding presence like Bale, but I've noticed there aren't a lot of straight up comedies among Christian's credits. In fact, I don't remember a single one.

Now I know why.

DANIEL DAY-LEWIS

As the only man in history to have won the best actor Oscar three times, Daniel Day-Lewis has more than cemented his place among film's all-time greats.

He also deserves a place in the eccentrics hall of fame for his extreme method actor antics when preparing for roles.

But the Daniel I encountered in real life may have been the strangest character of all.

We'll come back to that. First, let me run through just some of the lengths he's gone to in order to get into character for his films.

For historical drama *The Last of the Mohicans*, he lived off the land for six months and learned to hunt, kill, and skin animals for food.

He learned to write and paint with his toes for his role in *My Left Foot* as an artist suffering from cerebral palsy and refused to leave his wheel-chair for the duration of the shoot, insisting on being spoon fed and having people carry him in and out of the car each day.

To play a wrongly convicted prisoner for *In The Name of the Father*, he had himself locked in solitary confinement at an abandoned prison for two nights without any food or water.

There are countless more stories like this and, as far as I'm concerned, they demonstrate why Day-Lewis is widely considered the best—he pushes himself further than other actors for authenticity.

So it was with a great deal of enthusiasm and anticipation that I accepted an invitation to an advance screening of his latest film *Phantom Thread*— which had been announced as Daniel's final movie before retirement.

Taking my seat ten minutes before the screening I couldn't help but notice a bizarre looking figure sitting across the aisle from me. Tall and gangly and dressed in an all-black jogging suit, he had his hood up covering most of his face except for what looked like a crude fake stick-on nose.

Every two minutes a different flunky would come up to this figure, being careful not to say his name and asking if he needed anything. If this was a disguised Daniel Day-Lewis trying to keep a low profile, he wasn't exactly going the right way about it.

Eventually, the movie started but I couldn't tell you what happened for the first few minutes because I was too busy watching the oddball across the aisle. With the lights out he removed his hood and I could clearly tell it was the multiple Oscar winner, even with that big fake nose on.

Satisfied my assumptions were proved correct, I settled down to watch the film and was struggling to get into the slow-paced fashion designer drama when I was disturbed by a bright light to my right. Who on earth could be texting? That kind of behavior might happen at the multiplex every night but it's a big no-no at private screenings like this one.

I looked over and sure enough it was Daniel—merrily texting away. Maybe he was as bored by the film as me.

The biggest surprise, considering that he's played so many historical characters, was that Daniel Day-Lewis actually has a cell phone.

He left before the end of the movie. Maybe it was to avoid being recognized by the crowds as surely he couldn't hate the film as much as I did.

While *Phantom Thread* might not have been the best movie on which to end his career, it still landed him another Oscar nomination.

Having become so immersed in his characters, it feels like Daniel Day-Lewis has never shown us the real him. But that's fair enough—and probably the way he wants it.

ROBERT DUVALL and ROBERT DOWNEY, Jr.

Never in my wildest imagination would I have guessed the first words Robert Duvall said to me.

The veteran actor has been good in everything—right through from *To Kill a Mockingbird*, *The Godfather*, *Apocalypse Now*, *Days of Thunder*, and *Falling Down* to the latest movie I was to interview him for, *The Judge*.

So when we met in the back alley behind a movie theatre—we were due to walk in the rear exit for a Q&A with him and costar Robert Downey, Jr. after the screening—I enthusiastically told him how much I had enjoyed not just his performance in this film but in so many others down the years.

Hearing my English accent and nodding as I spoke, he sized me up and then said, "Do you like Michael Owen?"

That one took me by surprise. Could he mean Michael Owen the former Liverpool and England footballer? Who else could he mean?

"Yes," I replied. "Brilliant player."

Duvall was thrilled. "The best of all in my opinion. Never mind Ronaldo or Messi, Maradona or Pele, Michael Owen beats them all in my book."

This was awesome. As a huge fan of football, or soccer for my American readers, I warmed to my theme.

"What about that goal he scored against Argentina in the 1998 World Cup?"

Robert went into raptures about it.

In the midst of him acting act out the goal as if he had a ball at his feet, the other Robert, Downey Jr. showed up. We both barely acknowledged him.

Suddenly it was like me and Duvall were at the Stade Geoffrey-Guichard in St. Etienne, France, where that classic England v Argentina match was played rather than in the dark back alley outside a cinema in Santa Monica with Iron Man wondering if we had lost our minds.

With Downey feeling very left out of the conversation, which I imagine was something of a new experience for him, Duvall explained how he had become even more of a fan of the game after starring alongside former Scotland international Ally McCoist in a low-budget football movie called *A Shot at Glory* and now it was his second biggest passion after Argentinian tango dancing.

Who knew?

Much to my disappointment but probably to Robert Downey, Jr.'s relief, the back door of the movie theatre opened and the three of us were all ushered inside to talk about the making of *The Judge*, for which Duvall would receive his seventh Oscar nomination.

I can't remember much about that interview. But I can still remember every moment of Michael Owen's greatest goal as if it was yesterday. So can Robert Duvall.

KEANU REEVES

The first time I saw Keanu Reeves it was like encountering his Neo character from *The Matrix* because he was dressed just as he was in that movie with a long black trench coat over all black clothes.

But instead of demonstrating martial arts moves or dodging bullets in a simulated reality, he was photocopying a script in a printers' shop on Beverly Boulevard in West Hollywood.

It was surprising to me he wouldn't have someone to do that kind of task for him and then I remembered that, refreshingly, Reeves is one of the few Hollywood stars known for going out in public alone and without handlers.

I watched him leave and thought he would climb onto that Norton Commando motorbike I'd seen him riding in several photo shoots and roar off at speed.

Instead he got into a BMW car, carefully looked both ways, and joined the slow procession of L.A. traffic.

I wouldn't have to wait long to meet him because just a couple of weeks later I had been assigned thirty minutes to interview Keanu for a magazine.

I thought that would be plenty of time to get something newsworthy out of the star—but I had reckoned without his unusual way of answering questions.

Whenever I asked him something, a long pause would follow. Then Keanu would give a really long answer that veered off in so many directions that I'd forgotten what the original question was, or he would answer in just a couple of short phrases, or he would say nothing at all and there would be an uncomfortable silence that I wasn't sure if I was supposed to break—but usually did by asking another question.

Sometimes he seemed wise, other times aloof, I just didn't know what to make it of the enigma that is Keanu Reeves.

Having a thirty-five-year career in Hollywood is a remarkable achievement and so too is the ability to remain an inscrutable famous figure. Keanu has done both.

KIEFER SUTHERLAND

The nicest star I've ever met is Kiefer … at least when he's been sober.

In contrast to his take no prisoners *24* tough guy character Jack Bauer, in real life the actor is diffident and quiet.

But that all changes whenever he has some drink inside him—as I presume happened when he tackled the Christmas tree in the lobby of the Strand Palace Hotel in London.

I was there that headline-hitting night—it's the hotel where I usually stay in London—and in his defense, Kiefer went up to reception first, paid up front for the damages he was going to do, and then got into position.

Taking a long run up like an Olympic long jumper, he set off at pace and then launched himself through the air before crashing into the fully decorated Christmas tree knocking it to the ground and sending baubles and tinsel flying.

It must have seemed really funny to him. It just seemed weird to those of us enjoying a quiet coffee in the lobby and wondering what the hell he was doing.

He later explained to me it was done for a dare.

The incident was captured on camera for a documentary he was filming about his trip to London and I'm sure his assault on the tree is on YouTube if you ever want to watch it.

Kiefer's drinking eventually landed him in trouble with the law and he spent Christmas in prison a couple of years later. But it's pleasing to see he has stayed out of trouble and out of bars lately.

PAMELA ANDERSON

Pamela is another great survivor of the ups and downs of showbiz who I really like.

The former *Baywatch* babe is much smarter than her image might suggest and astutely aware of how she is perceived.

Pam is happy to play up to the ditzy blonde stereotype until someone tries to make fun of her and then the claws—and the brains—come out.

For example, I was at a press conference for her movie *Barb Wire* and one of the reporters mockingly asked her how many languages she could speak.

"About six or seven," she replied before calmly speaking sentences in German, French, Italian, and even Swedish to put the guy in his place.

I've met her a handful of times and each time has been a pleasure.

That's her on the cover of this book, in a great photo by Isaiah Mays, which perfectly captures the ultimate blonde just as she is—sexy, flirty, playful, and fun.

Now Isaiah is a world-class photographer but that shot is also terrific because Pamela knows how to deliver a perfect shot—the angle, the attitude, knowing where the light and shadow are. Not many stars are smart enough to figure all that out so well.

This book's cover girl taught me never to judge a book by its cover.

DANIEL CRAIG

The James Bond star is not the dour sourpuss many people imagine from his often downbeat print interviews.

He's actually a bit of a laugh once you get him going.

I've interviewed Daniel several times and find the best approach—especially on stage—is to make fun of him.

Over the years, he's been a good sport and relaxed into the joke as I've enquired about what I've called his "funny run" as 007 and his "Colonel Sanders accent" in *Knives Out*.

Maybe I shouldn't push things too much further as he does have a license to kill after all!

But I'm not too worried because as I learned when preparing to interview him at a *Skyfall* preview screening, even James Bond gets nervous like the rest of us.

When I told him there were two minutes to go until he was needed on stage, Daniel replied, "Just time for a cigarette then," and proceeded to light one up and smoke it quickly.

GEORGE LAZENBY

He may have only played James Bond once but George Lazenby has got enough stories to last a lifetime—as I found when interviewing the former 007 on stage at a special Los Angeles screening of his Bond film, *On Her Majesty's Secret Service.*

Most of the stories were about bedding Bond girls on set and even though he's now over eighty, the old rogue still has an eye for the ladies—as I could tell by the way his eyes were lingering on a fair few of the audience members that night.

But when we were chatting backstage—with no women around—he told me a tale even an ardent Bond fan like me had never known about him.

Turns out he used to be Russell Crowe's landlord.

"Russell lived in my spare room for three months when he first came to Los Angeles, didn't have any money and we shared the same agent. He kept auditioning for jobs in Hollywood but not getting hired because he kept doing the parts in an Aussie accent. I told him he had to do the parts in an American accent, he listened and now he's a huge star."

So the movie world has actually had a second major contribution from Lazenby—putting Russell Crowe on the path to stardom.

RUSSELL CROWE

I'm sure there are fights that go on all the time between movie stars and directors—but not usually at the after-party of a star-studded awards show.

Russell Crowe, however, does things slightly differently.

Until the violence started, it had seemed such a calm evening at the banquet following the 2002 BAFTA Film Awards where I was lucky enough to be on the press table at London's Grosvenor House hotel, tucking into a delicious meal and looking at the great and good of the movie industry enjoying their slap up feasts. Well, apart from Nicole Kidman who appeared to be eating just a raw carrot with a knife and fork.

The main topic of conversation on my table was general hilarity over the bizarre acceptance speech given by Russell Crowe who had deservedly won best actor for *A Beautiful Mind*. He had gone over the allotted time for acceptance speeches by, for whatever reason, reading out a poem called *Sanctity* by Patrick Kavanagh which was something about being a lover who managed to repel all women.

We wondered what the nation's TV viewers, who would by now be watching the tape delayed awards show in its broadcast version, were making of the unconventional speech.

Well it turned out they never heard most of it because the show's director, Malcolm Gerrie, had cut the poem part from the broadcast version of the show.

The first indication we got that it might turn out to be a controversial decision by Gerrie came when, of all people, pop star Sting came running into the banquet to warn Gerrie that Crowe was furious about having the poem cut and was on his way to sort him out.

Moments later Gerrie stepped into a side room and I guess Crowe must have caught up with him there judging from the commotion coming from inside.

I didn't see what was widely reported as being Crowe pinning the director against a wall and jabbing his finger repeatedly into his chest while berating him but I certainly heard the phrase, "You piece of shit, I'll make sure you never work in Hollywood."

Crowe stormed off into the night and hours later woke up to a storm of negative headlines.

It turned out he had intended the poem as a tribute to his gravely ill *Gladiator* costar and fellow hell-raiser Richard Harris, who had counted Kavanagh among his favorite poets.

He made a groveling apology to Gerrie in a personal phone call but the damage was done and many of my showbiz reporter colleagues feel the reason he failed to win the best actor Oscar for *A Beautiful Mind* that year was because he had lost his mind at the BAFTAs.

HENRY WINKLER

Anyone who has ever met him will tell you that *Happy Days* star Henry Winkler is the nicest man in show business.

He's very approachable to fans. Every day of his life several people give him the Fonz thumbs up and he gives it right back to them while smiling.

Henry is one of the few stars who does autograph conventions for the love rather than the money. He told me once at one of them, "What a lovely opportunity this is to meet all those people who adore seeing you and for me to make them happy in return."

I was not buying it. I'm not normally a cynical person but once imagined what if Henry Winkler was actually a secret serial killer who was kidnapping those fans and murdering them in his basement.

However, I don't think that's true. Especially after being the recipient of some true kindness from him.

I was once sitting at the same table as Henry for a charity event. I was only recently recovered from spinal surgery and wasn't supposed to be going out much but had wanted to attend because I believed in the cause. By this time, Henry was rising high on the success of his new sitcom *Barry*, which has deservedly won him a string of awards.

As the evening drew to a close, I started to be in great pain from sitting too long and when I got up from the table to excuse myself, my leg gave way under me and I collapsed.

Nobody else did anything but Henry was straight out of his chair, helped me up, and got me comfortable.

When it was obvious I still couldn't walk he went to fetch the strongest looking waiter at the hotel where the function was being held and he and

Henry then carried me out—an arm over each of their shoulders—to the front of the hotel.

There Henry summoned a taxi to take me home—what an absolute gentleman. I later thanked him for his kindness and he brushed off the praise and instead just thanked me for supporting the charity event we had been at. Legend.

ANTHONY DANIELS (C-3PO)

A long time ago in a galaxy far far away, I was in a dark storage room interviewing *Star Wars* actor Anthony Daniels.

The C-3PO star was at an HMV store for an autograph-signing session and to keep him away from the crowd that was forming, our pre-signing interview was done in the only available out of sight room there, a tiny storage closet where the light was broken.

We sat opposite each other in the dark on facing chairs and I could tell it was him because he spoke in a similar way to that high-pitched, fluctuating, and somewhat effeminate voice he uses as the golden android.

I started by telling Anthony what a fan I was of the *Star Wars* franchise and especially his part in it and was surprised when he replied, "Do you want to see it?"

And I started to get uncomfortable when he followed up by adding, "It's right here between my legs. Shall I get it out?"

I was nervously looking for the exit when he said, "I know you want to see it. I'm getting it out."

He reached between his legs, I heard a zip open, and he showed me his helmet.

I'm referring to the head of C-3PO which he carried with him in a hold all that was at his feet.

Apparently, he takes it with him to personal appearances and I was so pleased to be that close to a part of movie history and so I asked Anthony to touch it.

Then I happily polished his helmet and got on with the interview.

DAVID DUCHOVNY

When I met the leading man of *The X-Files*, chatting easily over the buffet at a showbiz party, he had seemed funny, well read, and smart. I wasn't surprised to learn David Duchovny had earned a masters degree in English Literature from Yale University.

But I was questioning if he was actually a complete idiot when I later got approached by a TV network for help with finding the actor's dream present.

It had been explained to me that this satellite TV channel which screened his show in the UK had wanted him to fly to London to promote the latest series of the show with British press and when he proved reluctant to do it they had decided to buy Duchovny a gift to persuade him. It's called "talent management" supposedly.

Word came back to me that what literature fan David has asked for was a first edition of the complete works of Shakespeare, autographed by the Bard of Avon himself.

Now this is where I thought he must be moronic because as most of us literature scholars know, all of Shakespeare's manuscripts were lost long ago and the first collected plays were not published until 1623, and as Shakespeare had died seven years before that, there was certainly no autographed first edition.

But then it occurred to me that Duchovny must know that and this was just a polite or clever way of turning down the press trip. Or maybe it was a test of how far the channel would go to please him.

I had also learned that it was not the done thing to question or say no to stars but instead try and get as close to what they wanted as possible. So my mission began.

My first stop was an antiquarian book shop in the West End of London where I had often browsed the hugely collectable rare titles but never been able to afford them.

However, as a TV station was footing the bill I felt confident I'd come out of there with something worthwhile. When I explained the situation to the shop manager he first fell about laughing but then recovered his composure to outline my options.

He said there were a handful of copies in the world of the First Folios, the original collection of Shakespeare's 36 plays, but most were in museums and on the rare occasion one became available at auction they sold for between $4.5 million and $6 million.

So I settled instead for the oldest and dustiest looking complete works of Shakespeare book in the shop—which cost well over a grand.

But that still left the question of the autograph. Next stop was the British Museum where they keep a document signed by the Bard in their permanent collection.

The curator told me only six autographs from William Shakespeare exist and all are to be found on legal documents. He added that Shakespeare wrote with a wobbly hand and some experts thought that might indicate he suffered from a tremor.

This was good information for the final part of my mission. I remembered that on a school trip to Stratford-upon-Avon there had been a guy dressed as Shakespeare in a tourist museum who would sign his name with a quill pen. Wondering if he was still there, and being on an expenses account, I caught a train to Stratford.

Sure enough, I found him. I told fake Shakespeare the story which he found highly enjoyable—and it turned out he was a huge fan of David's *X-Files* character, Fox Mulder. I asked him to sign my complete works of

Shakespeare book with a quill pen and make sure the signature looked wobbly to add an air of authenticity.

He asked me, smiling, "Should I sign it 'To David'...," and I replied, "No, we might be pushing our luck."

Armed with my signed book, the mission was complete. I explained to the TV company I had the next best thing to the real thing, they seemed pleased, and I sent the gift off to Duchovny via *The X-Files* office with a letter and another plea to come to England for the press trip.

I've no idea what he thought of the present but I expect it amused him because a couple of weeks later David Duchovny was giving all those British press interviews! I'm also convinced he had no idea what I'd been through to get the present.

There are more things on heaven and earth, David, that are dreamt of in your philosophy.

MARGOT ROBBIE

Margot is every bit as smart as she is talented and beautiful. I say that partly because she was wise enough to hire me for a special assignment.

The Aussie actress was preparing to produce as well as star in the ice skater biopic, *I, Tonya*, and in order to get the movie made was looking to raise funds at the American Film Market.

That's an annual industry event in L.A.'s coastal town of Santa Monica attended by distributors, investors, and producers from around the world—so she'd certainly come to the right place.

Her idea was to have me interview her and director Craig Gillespie on stage about the planned film and they would make it sound so exciting and commercial that the invited audience would immediately empty their pockets of the $11 million needed to make the movie.

Everything was done in style—especially the amazing limousine which was sent to pick me up from home and take me to and from the interview.

And Margot was lovely—just super down to earth and very funny like so many Australians I've met over the years.

She proved a great interview and so did Craig. Heck, I was ready to invest my Q&A fee into the film there and then, it sounded so good.

The next clever move came afterward when anyone potentially interested in investing in the film could meet Margot privately backstage to briefly discuss it—and get a selfie with the actress as well.

But to make sure everyone was serious the selfies cost $50 with all the proceeds going toward the film's budget.

Anyway, it all worked like a dream because the money was found unusually quickly to fund the film and as the world now knows the movie, in which Margot played controversial ice skater Tonya Harding, was a big success earning $54 million at the global box office and three Oscar nominations including one for Robbie as best actress.

Anytime you need me again Margot, you have my number.

SANDRA BULLOCK

You won't be surprised to know that Sandra Bullock is just as brilliant, funny, and adorable in real life as she often is on screen.

But what you might not know is how much love she has in her heart for disabled dogs.

As a pet lover myself I enjoy talking to her about what I hesitate to call her four-legged friends. Because the pooches she adopts from rescue shelters rarely have four legs.

Whenever the shelter gets a dog that has a limb missing or some other special needs, they call her.

"Any dog that is missing something is welcome in my house," says Sandra.

When I last spoke to her she'd adopted one with three legs, one with two legs and one missing an eye.

As well as being a Hollywood movie star, she owns a bakery in Austin, Texas, and is considerate of her canine visitors as there's a shaded area outside where dogs can drink water and relax while their owners enjoy cakes and a coffee inside.

Great actress and a great heart.

CHAPTER 3:

THOSE NO LONGER WITH US

MICHAEL JACKSON

Perhaps the biggest story I have covered as a showbiz reporter was the death of Michael Jackson, for which I was live on BBC radio for many hours describing the scene outside the Los Angeles hospital where he was declared dead.

I was the first reporter on the scene but only by a stroke of pure coincidence—as I happened to be eating lunch at a restaurant around the corner when I was phoned with the tip that the King of Pop had died at UCLA Medical Center. Immediately I abandoned my cheeseburger, grabbed my phone and press card, and prepared to broadcast to my home nation.

It was a surreal experience to be reporting on Michael's death because the flamboyant figure had been so much part of our lives. Mine included. I'd reported on 'Jacko' for years, met him twice in a pair of brief backstage exchanges of pleasantries, had been to Neverland, his former housekeeper, Adrian McManus, was a friend of mine, and I'd encountered various members of the Jackson family over the years.

Having seen coverage of the death of Princess Diana twelve years earlier, I was expecting to be describing a similarly solemn scene this time—but how wrong I was. As the crowds gathered on June 25, 2009, to pay their respects, it was almost a carnival atmosphere.

Maybe that's because the hospital was on the campus of UCLA University and there were lots of boisterous students around or maybe they just grieve differently for their idols in America.

But I remember describing fans in a conga line outside dancing to *Billie Jean* while nurses from the hospital formed an impromptu choir singing *Man in the Mirror* to the TV cameras while each wearing one surgical glove.

Within ninety minutes of his death the souvenir t-shirt sellers showed up trying to sell their quickly printed Michael Jackson RIP t-shirts to the gathering crowds. I remember one such tradesman talking a cop out of moving him on by giving him the officer six free t-shirts to look the other way.

It was a similar circus days later when I attended Jackson's public memorial service held at Staples Center, the sports stadium and concert venue in downtown Los Angeles.

The circus word is used deliberately because there was even a parade of Barnum and Bailey elephants outside before the service and countless Michael Jackson impersonators dancing, singing, and posing for pictures.

Inside a string of stars took to the stage to pay tribute including Mariah Carey, Stevie Wonder, Usher, and Smokey Robinson—and then for some reason, *Britain's Got Talent* contestant Shaheen Jafargholi—before the Jackson brothers, all wearing a single white glove, carried out the casket. As funerals go, it was quite a show.

JIMMY STEWART

The first interview I ever did in Hollywood was one of the last interviews given by the legendary star of *It's a Wonderful Life*, *Harvey*, *Mr Smith Goes to Washington,* and so many other classics.

What a thrill to meet Jimmy Stewart who, of course, looked so much older in person than the figure I remembered from all those black and white movies on TV.

It was at a fundraising benefit to build a museum for air force heroes of World War II—whose number included Stewart himself as he had served in that conflict.

The veteran actor looked frail but was a total gentleman and a class act—unlike me who, being new to celebrity interviewing, was a wide-eyed rookie in the presence of such greatness.

My first mistake was to speak to him like I tended to speak to most elderly people in those days—by raising my voice.

I boomed out my first question, "You were in *It's a Wonderful Life* so what's been the most wonderful part of your life?"

Then I kept going with questions in similarly high volume like, "When you acted in *Harvey*, did you start seeing imaginary rabbits in real life just like your character in the movie?"

Jimmy graciously answered all the questions and put up with this human loudspeaker act for about fifteen minutes before asking for a halt and patiently asking me, "Why are you shouting, son? I may be old but I'm not deaf!"

CHARLTON HESTON

Right after our interview, Jimmy Stewart was kind enough to introduce me to another classic star attending that same event, Charlton Heston.

Introducing me, he said, "Sandro, I'd like you to meet a friend of mine. This is Chuck Heston."

His fellow superstar thrust out his right hand for me to shake. I should have just taken it and said: "Pleased to meet you, sir."

But I was new to the Hollywood scene, felt a little starstruck, froze for a moment and had a weird flashback.

I instantly thought back to the first time I'd seen Heston—in that fantastic movie *Planet of the Apes*.

Thinking it would impress him or make him laugh I decided in the spur of the moment to quote one of his memorable lines from that film.

Stepping out of the way of his offered handshake, I said, "Get your stinking paws off me you God damn dirty ape."

Instead of smiling or laughing, Charlton Heston gave me a look of pity and turned away.

FRANK SINATRA

I was at one of the last concerts Frank ever performed—and I'll never forget it.

Unfortunately, that night Sinatra forgot most of the words.

Ol' Blue Eyes also told the same anecdotes repeatedly, sang the same songs twice, and introduced his conductor son Frank Jr. multiple times.

The audience members, myself included, didn't seem to mind as it was just so amazing to be in the presence of the silver toupee wearing superstar.

This was in 1993 … twenty-two years after he had announced his retirement! Frank had done a thousand comeback/farewell concerts since then.

But that night we knew the *My Way* singer was facing the final curtain.

Luckily, I got to see him again under better circumstances eighteen months later.

This was at a celebrity golf tournament in Palm Desert, California, where I fired a few questions at the great singer. I asked mainly about golf rather than music which is presumably why he was happy to talk and he seemed in really good spirits.

I'm so glad that was the last time I saw him, rather than my final memory of Frank being that concert where for once he fell short of his sensational standards.

Frank passed away in 1998 but the legend leaves a legacy like no other.

He continued to intrigue me so much that I wrote a play about him, *Marilyn and Sinatra*, which played to full houses around the world. I was soon to learn that even from beyond the grave, Francis Albert Sinatra still exerts a huge influence.

On our opening night in New York, a bunch of mobsters who had revered Frank were sitting on the front row. At the after-party, one of the square nosed tough guys approached me. That was a nervous moment.

To my huge relief, he said, "Thanks for not dissing Frank in the show. If you had done, me and the boys might have had to have a few words."

WHITNEY HOUSTON

As one of the last people to see Whitney Houston alive, and being a big fan of her music, the singer's death hit me pretty hard.

I had been doing interviews with other performers at the Grammy Awards rehearsals two days before the tragic news broke and had seen Whitney in the distance that afternoon and remember being sad she wasn't being made available to the media.

Exactly forty-eight hours later she was found dead in the bathtub of room 434, her suite at the Beverly Hilton Hotel, just steps from where I live in Beverly Hills.

That great talent had ultimately fallen victim to the demons which had derailed her life and career.

But the demonic behavior which followed from people the world has never heard of made things even sadder.

For many months afterward, various insensitive guests would book into room 434 and post on social media sick joke photos of them posing in the bathtub where Whitney died.

When they started tagging the hotel in those posts the Beverly Hilton knew it had a problem and 434 was removed as a room, stripped of its furniture and used for storage rather than continuing as a macabre tourist attraction.

I walk or drive past that hotel every day—and still think of Whitney each time.

When I'd first met her while she was promoting *The Bodyguard*, she was so full of life and everything seemed possible.

In the end this was yet another great star who burned out under the addictions and toxic temptations which are such a scourge on celebrity and society.

JOHN THAW

Inspector Morse remains, at least in my view, the best TV detective character ever.

No murderer in Oxford could evade capture from the beer swilling, Jaguar driving, classical-music-loving grumpy cop played so perfectly by the late John Thaw.

I would see John once a year at the press launch of every new series of Morse—an experience he would clearly enjoy about as much as the trip to the dentist.

Leaving costar Kevin Whately to take the majority of press conference questions he would endure the publicity process then disappear without ever any pleasantries to us journalists.

If you've ever seen the series six episode *Happy Families*, where Morse is put before the media, the uncomfortable result is just like one of those real-life media gatherings for the show.

But at the press call for the last ever Morse episode, *The Remorseful Day*, there was a very different atmosphere from the start.

It was no secret that John was very ill. A heavy smoker from the age of twelve, he would soon pass away from throat cancer.

After the press conference, a few of us reporters were milling around enjoying the buffet lunch provided by the TV company when something happened which had never happened before at the Morse launches. John Thaw came over to speak to me.

He said, "Listen, I've seen you at the previous launches and we haven't spoken before but maybe you'd like an exclusive quote on the final episode."

I replied, "How kind. I'm Sandro, big fan. I guess my question is how does it feel to say goodbye to a character which has meant so much to you and so many millions of viewers around the world?"

Thaw, looked hesitant and then came out with it: "Before I answer that, here's the deal … can you first go to the shop around the corner and buy me a packet of twenty cigarettes?"

Indicating the TV company executives over his shoulder, he added: "They won't let me have any."

Well this was tempting, I really wanted to get the exclusive quote but at the same time I didn't want to kill one of the nation's TV heroes.

I had to explain to John Thaw that I didn't think that would be appropriate.

He gave a polite smile, nodded, and turned away.

The last time I saw John Thaw he was approaching another journalist at the launch and saying, "Listen, I've seen you at the previous launches and we haven't spoken before but…."

ROBIN WILLIAMS

I cohosted a memorial event for Robin Williams at the world-famous Chinese Theatre on Hollywood Boulevard after his tragic death.

Having interviewed him a dozen times and been one of his many fans, the event was an opportunity to grieve his loss and celebrate his life.

When the fabulous actor and funnyman committed suicide, I had been heartbroken but somehow not that surprised.

Each time I interviewed him, I always felt the smile on his clowning face was masking deep hurt. Sometimes that mask would slip and he'd let you in to his pain.

The most telling and honest conversation we had came when I asked him why he had moved out of Los Angeles to Northern California.

Robin explained he had done it to escape the entertainment business being all around him.

He said: "It becomes about where you are on the Hollywood food chain. Whether you're the number one star or number seventy-five or number two thousand it's never easy. When you're coming up you want to be number one and when you're number one there's always someone coming up to challenge you."

I had never thought about fame like that before but it made a lot of sense.

At the memorial service, we screened my favorite film of his, *Dead Poets Society*, a movie which follows a beautiful spirit who ultimately takes his own life.

I still miss Robin. Listeners to my podcast, *Who's the Best*, voted him the best comedian of all time. Can't disagree with that.

LESLIE NIELSEN

The *Naked Gun* funnyman was committed to raising a smile off-screen as well as on.

He carried a fart machine with him everywhere and would let it off at the most unexpected times.

I didn't know about the special tiny device he had hidden in his hand when I first interviewed him.

I was telling Leslie about how my late grandmother had adored him, calling him the most handsome man who ever lived, and was talking about her love for the actor right to the end.

While I was telling this heartfelt story, Nielsen was nodding sadly and "farting" like crazy.

I mentioned this to a fellow journalist afterward who enlightened me that I'd fallen into Leslie's trap.

Apparently, he loved nothing more than seeing journalists keep a straight face while he pretended to have passed gas.

Nielsen had started his career as a serious actor and that made him credible while delivering such straight-faced comedy in *Airplane, The Naked Gun,* and other later projects.

He was clearly hilarious in real life too, and I'm honored to have been fooled by his crappy trick.

ELIZABETH TAYLOR

It's never a good idea to upset a legend.

They are too used to getting things their own way.

Elizabeth Taylor had shown up to a swanky Beverly Hills Hotel function room to receive a lifetime achievement award—but hadn't realized those of us in the audience waiting to see her were being served a chicken dinner before the speeches.

That didn't work for Liz. Apparently, she was on a schedule and not too keen to wait around for her trophy.

So she decided to make her way through the ballroom to the stage to grab the award and launch straight into the speech.

But the injured icon was in a wheelchair at the time and set off wheeling herself forward from the back of the room with all the subtlety of a bull in a china shop.

Seeing her coming I was able to dive out of the way just in time but my friend Christine sitting next to me wasn't so lucky and Liz's wheelchair went right over her left foot.

Christine was wearing Gucci platforms and as she winced from having her foot run over by the rampaging legend, Liz looked over her shoulder and said, "Sorry about that dear, hope you're alright," and kept on going.

And doesn't that just sum up Elizabeth Taylor's philosophy? Whether she was stealing close friend Debbie Reynolds' husband Mike Fisher, or stealing a march at an awards show, Liz never let anything stop her.

PATRICK McGOOHAN

Let me tell you about the time I nearly killed one of my show-biz heroes....

The unlucky recipient of my starstruck stupidity was Patrick McGoohan, reclusive star of the much repeated but never bettered 1960s TV series *The Prisoner*.

The hidden meanings behind the masterpiece about a secret agent held captive in a mysterious village continue to fascinate fans, especially as McGoohan, who was the show's creator as well as star, provided no answers in the show's final episode.

That so annoyed viewers at the time that he felt the need to flee Britain for a new life in America to escape their fury and he had largely avoided the spotlight ever since, refusing requests from fans and interviewers to explain what his creation was all about.

I was one of those fans who longed for the opportunity to spend a few minutes in the presence of the elusive actor to gather some clues—but never thought I would see him.

Then one day I was shopping in Santa Monica, California, with my friend Tiffany and we were walking back to the multistory car park where we had parked on the roof when I noticed a scruffy vagrant behind us as we headed to the elevators.

Turning around, I could sense there was something somehow trou-bling and even sinister about this wild-eyed and hairy old tramp and that uneasy feeling caused me to increase the pace of my walking and press the lift call button several times.

Just as the elevator doors opened and we stepped inside, the old man stuck out an arm to hold the door open. Damn. Then a well-dressed woman around his age and someone else I took to be her daughter walked in as well, and we all shared the lift together.

I stared at the floor, as is my way in elevators, until the doors opened on the third floor and the two women and the old man got out. It seemed they were together. Just before the doors closed on us I took my first real look at the mystery man—and froze.

It was him! Yes, older and scruffier than I remember but opening the car door for what must be his wife and daughter.

I remember as the doors closed Tiffany turned to me and said, "What's wrong? You look like you're having a menopausal hot flush!"

Excitedly, I jabbered: "Do you realize who that was?" She was nonplussed. "Patrick McGoohan!"

Tiffany replied, "Patrick Mc Who?"

I then gave a rather hurried explanation of the man and the mystery and explained this was going to be my only ever chance to meet him and I had to take it.

She was looking at me despairingly on the walk to the car as I explained he already had the jump on us by being three floors lower down—so I told Tiffany I was going to run after him and confront my idol.

Used to such over-the-top dumbness from me at this point, my friend shrugged her shoulders and said she'd pick me up outside on the street whenever I had done what I needed to do.

I set off running.

By the time I got to the third floor there was no sign of McGoohan's car. He must already be heading to the ground floor exit. So I increased my pace.

As I ran down the ramps and spotted Patrick's car in the distance I started to formulate a plan. He would have to stop at the barrier by the pay booth to display his ticket. At that point, I would get in front of Patrick and give him the "Be seeing you" sign from *The Prisoner*.

As any fan of the show knows, that was a particular hand gesture, based on the Christian sign of the fish, with which characters in the show greeted each other.

In my addled mind, I thought if McGoohan saw me doing that he would be so impressed to see such a devoted fan of his work he would invite me home with the family for tea and talk about *The Prisoner*.

I didn't quite make it in time to catch him at the barrier. Nearly exhausted at this point, I'm not the fittest to be fair, I caught up with the car just as it was going through the barrier and, at the wheel, McGoohan was looking left and right preparing to turn into the street.

What I did next was very foolish and dangerous but there's a kind of mania that comes over you as a fan.

I stepped out in front of the car, with a big smile on my face, and greeted the driver with my "Be Seeing You" gesture.

He saw me alright. In fact he swerved the car to avoid me and so nearly had an accident. Stopped in the middle of the street, his car facing the wrong way, McGoohan had a face like thunder.

It seemed best to make a sharp exit at this point.

Luckily, I then saw Tiffany's car exiting the parking structure and heading in my direction. I quickly ran alongside the car, indicated desperately for her to unlock the passenger door, she did so and I dived in.

"Go! Go! Go!" I yelled. And she did.

We raced off as she asked me if I was pleased with myself. Not really.

McGoohan died the next year after a short illness. I'm so sorry I never got to meet him under better circumstances.

However, I did subsequently get to meet his actress daughter Catherine at an event celebrating *The Prisoner*. She was lovely and spoke so warmly about her dad. I wisely didn't mention I was the idiot who ran in front of his car that day. Fans like me do the silliest things sometimes.

CHAPTER 4:

BRITISH STARS

BENEDICT CUMBERBATCH

B enedict was desperate to go to the toilet.

I could see it in the *Sherlock* star's face from the moment he arrived backstage at an L.A. screening room with one minute to go until our scheduled Q&A with an industry audience.

Welcoming him and the four female publicists he had with him, I quickly ran through the format of the upcoming interview and asked if he had any questions.

Benedict turned pleadingly to his handlers and asked, "Have I time to go to the toilet?"

They immediately ruled it out, explaining there were no facilities backstage and he'd have to walk through the audience to visit the one at the back of the room. And anyway, they were on a schedule.

Benedict's look of resignation seemed to say, "I guess I can hold it."

That was good enough for me and so I bounded out on stage to introduce him and all seemed to be fine.

He told great stories, including one about how he had spent half a year in a Buddhist monastery in India and how that experience helped keep him calm under the pressures of showbiz.

But even that zen attitude couldn't help him as the pang to pee suddenly came back.

Benedict was too polite and clearly didn't want to risk any embarrassment by asking to be excused to spend a penny.

First, he started crossing and uncrossing his legs on stage, then a look of impending alarm came across his face, and as I still wasn't wrapping up the interview he started peppering his answers with signals that he really needed to go to the toilet, even saying at that point he was "flushed" with success.

Eventually, I got the message, called a halt to proceedings early and Benedict politely shook my hand and thanked me before racing out down the back stairs, out of the building and toward wherever he could relieve himself.

HUGH GRANT

The last time I saw Hugh Grant, he was surrounded by seven gorgeous models and told me, "I'm trying to keep a low profile."

He's clearly as much a master of irony as he is a master of comedic acting!

It was at the Edinburgh Fringe Festival where I spotted him in the row behind me at a comedy show about the British press.

I said hello but he shushed me in case anyone else there should recognize him.

The baseball cap he wore displaying the logo of Malibu restaurant *Moonshadows* provided some disguise I suppose. But the seven bombshells beside him were a little inconspicuous.

Talking of Hugh's love of the ladies, I'll never forget covering that huge story when he was arrested for soliciting a prostitute named Divine Brown on Sunset Boulevard.

I spent the day after that incident putting up wanted style posters on the famous street urging anyone who knew Divine's whereabouts to call me and claim a cash reward if their information resulted in me getting the first interview with Divine.

Unbeknownst to me, another paper's reporter already had her spirited away and had bought up her story. But there is a constant reminder of Hugh Grant's dalliance with Divine Brown on the corner where it happened.

Now on that site is a British theme pub called The Pikey where Divine Brown's framed mug shot from that night hangs outside the ladies toilet while Hugh's mug shot is just outside the men's.

TOM HIDDLESTON

I probably did more damage to Tom Hiddleston's career than his headline hitting brief romance with Taylor Swift.

That's because I advised him what to say in his 2017 Golden Globes acceptance speech for best actor in a TV miniseries, awarded for his brilliant performance in *The Night Manager*.

That's right, the toe-curlingly embarrassing speech he later had to publicly apologize for.

Tom is a lovely, fun, approachable guy and at a party the day before the ceremony I was telling him how *The Night Manager* had impacted people right around the world even to the point where it distracted so many from their troubles.

He seemed very pleased with this so I suggested that could be the theme of his speech if he won, which I felt sure he would.

Tom took the idea and ran with it. Ran too far as it turned out.

My idea was that his speech should sound grateful. Not completely self-serving like it did.

As he took the stage at the Globes, Hiddleston revealed a group of doctors doing relief work in South Sudan had "binge watched" the spy series. I cringed as he said, "The idea that I could provide some relief and entertainment for the people who work for UNICEF, Medecins Sans Frontieres, and the World Food Programme, who are fixing the world in the places where it is broken, made me immensely proud."

The reaction on social media was rapid and not pretty. Tom received so much abuse online that he was forced into posting an apology for the speech on his Facebook page the next day.

"I completely agree that my speech at the Golden Globes last night was inelegantly expressed," he wrote. "In truth, I was very nervous and my words just came out wrong."

I was just relieved he didn't add, "In my defense, Sandro Monetti told me to do it!"

ROB BRYDON

I've been avoiding Rob Brydon for a couple of years now—and will continue to do so. Let me explain why.

I'm a big admirer of his work, especially in *Gavin and Stacey* and also on *The Trip* with Steve Coogan, where he so perfectly impersonates Al Pacino and other stars.

When Rob was in L.A. rehearsing to host an awards show, the Welsh funnyman approached me conspiratorially.

"Sandro, I hear you know Al Pacino...."

It's true, I do having interviewed Al a few times and always got along well with the acting legend.

So I replied, "That's right, Rob."

He continued, "I wonder if I could ask you a favor.... Could you find out if Al knows who I am? Has he seen my impersonations of him and what does he think of them?"

It seemed a bit odd and a little needy. But so am I, so I accepted the mission.

We agreed I would check it out and let Rob know the answer the following night when he would be hosting the awards show.

Minutes later I called Al's best friend and asked him if Pacino was aware of Rob Brydon.

"Absolutely not," came the reply. "Those of us who know him all know about *The Trip* but Al isn't really aware of a lot of pop culture and just doesn't care about things like that. He only sees impressions of him when they are played to him on talk shows, otherwise there's no interest at all so it's a definite no."

That was no surprise to me. But instantly I knew Rob would be crushed he wasn't on his hero's radar. I couldn't tell him the truth. But I don't tell lies either. So I knew the perfect solution: avoid him.

The next night at the Beverly Hilton Hotel where the awards show was taking place, Rob Brydon kept spotting me from across the room and I would wave back but kept avoiding him.

He flew home to Britain the next morning and I got away with not having to deliver the bad news. I still haven't.

If you're reading this Rob, I'm sorry but Al Pacino has never heard of you.

HELEN MIRREN

Helen Mirren was swearing like a sailor.

"That poster makes it look like a movie about two old bastards fucking," she declared as I walked in ahead of our interview.

She was speaking to a publicist for the movie *The Last Station* who had been seeking her opinion on the promotional image for the historical drama in which she played the wife of Russian author Leo Tolstoy.

It was a surprising introduction for me to an actress so regal in roles like The Queen and many other classics.

But as I was soon to find, Helen has a great sense of humor and uses very colorful language off-screen.

Not only does she swear like a sailor, she's tattooed like one too.

At that first meeting I couldn't help but notice she had a tattoo on her left hand—interlocking letters which are apparently a symbol meaning "love thy neighbor."

When I asked about it she explained she got it when very drunk once in the 1970s and ever since has covered up the tat with makeup for screen roles.

RUSS ABBOT

The first celebrity interview I ever got in print was with one of the top comedy stars of my childhood, Russ Abbot.

I delivered newspapers before and after school as a thirteen-year-old and the TV star's house was on my round.

So one day I slipped a note around his evening paper explaining that I was a big fan and would like to feature him in the school magazine I was starting and if he'd be interested would he please answer the questions on the other side of this note.

Well, when I got to his house the next morning, the note was sticking out of the letterbox with his answers all filled in. How incredibly kind.

So far I've never had the chance to meet Russ Abbot to thank him for his kindness but that small gesture set me on the way to a celebrity journalism career.

My independent school magazine—far more gossipy and fun than the stuffy official one—launched with an exclusive Russ Abbot interview, plus some scurrilous gossip about a few of the teachers. It became very popular with my schoolmates and my path in life was set.

DAVID JASON and NICHOLAS LYNDHURST

Meeting the stars of that fantastic British sitcom *Only Fools and Horses* was a real letdown.

When you love characters as much as working-class heroes Del Boy and Rodney Trotter, you hope the actors who play them will be very similar in real life.

So to find that David Jason seemed very serious was just as disappointing as discovering the actor who plays his brother appeared really posh.

But, as I reflected after that press call for the show's final episode, what makes them such wonderful actors is that they seem so convincing as other people.

Even after all these years, I still think actors are going to be like the characters they play. But it's so rarely the case.

VANESSA FELTZ

Soul singer Barry White was the boss of the bedroom, a man whose music was constantly voted into the top ten songs to play while making love.

Inhibitions flew away at just the sound of his sexy voice—as I found when attending one of his last concerts, an intimate private London gathering for celebrities and journalists.

For some reason all bags and possessions had to be checked in at the cloakroom before entry into the small showroom but a good reporter is never without his phone so I stuffed mine down the front of my trousers—a fact which will become relevant soon.

Anyway, the show started and Barry packed the dance floor right away with *Can't Get Enough of Your Love* and I was gently grooving along with my journalistic colleague Emily and enjoying the show when it happened.

Barry launched into his most romantic hit *You're the First, the Last, My Everything* when I suddenly heard a cry of "Sandrooooooooo" from the other end of the room and looked to see who was heading toward me.

The dance floor parted as TV and radio presenter Vanessa Feltz, with a white dress on her body and a look of lust on her face, stampeded across it, barging Emily out of the way and started what I can only describe as dirty dancing next to me, bumping and grinding for all she was worth.

Overcome by Barry White's music and the moment, she thrust against my groin, felt the hardness of the mobile phone down there, mistook it for something else and purred, "Ooh Sandro, I never knew you cared."

Picking Emily off the floor and slowly edging away, I quickly disappeared into the crowd before things got any more heated.

I saw Vanessa again a few weeks later in Ireland when she had invited me to a press launch for her new TV talk show at the Blarney Stone, a block of limestone built into the battlements of a castle near Cork which, according to a tradition dating back to 1446, is supposed the give the gift of the gab (great eloquence) to anyone who kisses it.

Vanessa was looking forward to locking lips with the old rock as a good luck gesture for her new show until I told her some rumor the crew had shared with me that, according to another tradition, local pranksters liked to urinate on it at night and get amused about all the people who will be kissing it the next day.

But the host was not to be deterred and although screwing her face up a bit while doing so, kissed the famous stone.

Its magic must have worked because nearly twenty years later Vanessa is still a popular and successful broadcaster.

MICHAEL SHEEN

I'm proud of finally introducing the *Carry On* films to America—and I have that great actor Michael Sheen to thank for helping me do it.

He and I are both fans of the bawdy British comedy franchise—Michael played one of its stars, Kenneth Williams, in the biopic *Fantabulosa*—and wanted the movie fans of our adopted home city of Los Angeles to see what they had been missing.

Much to our honor, the American Cinematheque—a great organization which screens popular old films from around the world—agreed to host our special *Carry On* night.

Intrigued that this thirty-one-film series of lowbrow comedies was largely unknown and unreleased stateside they promoted it well and their Aero cinema was packed for the double bill event.

We screened *Fantabulosa* followed by innuendo laden side-splitter *Carry On Camping* and in between I interviewed Michael on stage about these wacky movies he'd been raised on and what they meant to him and so many others.

Michael, so great as Tony Blair, David Frost, Brian Clough, Chris Tarrant, and every other role he's ever played, is a warm, witty, and wonderful man whose enthusiasm for the *Carry On* institution carried over to the audience.

News of the popular event went worldwide and a few days later I was delighted to receive a lovely email from the son of Sid James, a comic actor with a trademark dirty laugh who appeared in 19 of the 31 *Carry On* films, getting top billing in 17 of them—including *Carry On Camping*.

He told me it had always been Sid's dream to be in a movie seen in Hollywood and wanted to thank Michael and me for making that dream come true.

We don't often recognize some of the happiest moments of our life when we are living them but sitting with Michael Sheen in Los Angeles seeing how an audience which had largely never seen *Carry On* were lapping up the cheap laughs was absolutely lovely.

ROGER DEAKINS

The largest Q&A I ever did saw fourteen guests on the same stage—the cast and moviemakers from Oscar winner *No Country for Old Men*.

It was going quite well with fascinating insight and comments from the various guests, who included Javier Bardem, Josh Brolin, and the Coen Brothers, and then halfway through something very strange happened.

A silver-haired man of nearly sixty, wearing a black leather jacket, suddenly wandered on stage, took a seat on the end, and joined the panel.

Problem was I had no idea who he was. While Javier Bardem was answering the previous question, I was staring at the interloper trying to place who he might have played in the movie. Was he one of the cops? Not sure. What on earth was I going to ask him?

I decided it was best to go with something neutral and open ended in the hope his answer would reveal to me who he was.

I said: "To the newcomer on the panel, what was your … hardest challenge on the film?"

When he replied, "As a cinematographer, there are so many challenges…." I immediately relaxed.

Clearly this was Roger Deakins, the greatest cinematographer in the business.

I dodged a possible bullet there, and said, "thank you, Roger Deakins" after his answer and continued with the panel.

I've so admired his work since on projects like *Skyfall, Blade Runner 2049,* and *1917* and when we met again early in 2020—at a reception for British Oscar nominees—I asked Roger what he was working on now.

He replied, "The garden fence."

I said, "Oh, I've not heard of that movie. What's it about?"

Roger clarified, "No, it's not a movie. I'm between jobs so I'm painting the fence in my garden."

Well, he's such a visual master that I'll bet that fence is perfectly lit and looks absolutely stunning.

TERRY WAITE

One of Britain's most famous hostages, Terry Waite, was held captive in Lebanon for 1,763 days—most of them in solitary confinement.

The peace envoy never knew such solitude again until he showed up at a bookstore at L.A.'s Beverly Center shopping mall to sign copies of his book, *Taken on Trust*, and absolutely nobody showed up.

Nobody apart from me that is.

Having been moved by his story and campaigned for his release, I was excited to meet him.

Before joining the non-existent queue for his signature, I browsed around the other books in the store and couldn't help noticing what Terry Waite was doing while waiting for customers to show up.

He started reading a copy of his own book.

While hugely famous back in Britain, it appeared his celebrity had not reached the United States—but at least he had one fan there.

I interrupted his reading to ask him to sign my book and he was delighted to do so—and we had a long chat.

There was a lot to talk about because, would you believe, when Waite was held captive in Lebanon, I was renting an old room of his from his family.

I'd already moved on to somewhere else by the time he was freed so at least there was no awkward discussion to be had about giving him his old place back.

Terry has since become a lecturer, broadcaster and formed a support group for families of hostages. I've still got my signed book and it's well worth a read.

As were his opinions when the coronavirus crisis hit. As someone used to being isolated, due to his hostage experiences, he urged people to change their mindset saying we were not STUCK at home but SAFE at home.

His advice was: be grateful for what you have—shelter, home, possessions—form a structure for the day, read and be creative.

Thanks for your advice Terry—I wrote this book during the lockdown.

SIMON COWELL

For someone who has made his name making pop stars famous, it's remarkable how little Simon Cowell loves the music business.

Not only did I see not a single gold disc on the walls at a visit to his London home, I only noticed two albums in his collection—old time crooners Tony Bennett and Frank Sinatra by the way.

When I later visited him at his even more luxurious Los Angeles house, there wasn't even one album.

But as Simon explained to me, he has an ear for catchy pop music but is no particular fan of it.

After success as a record executive, he became a star for his withering put-downs on talent shows like *American Idol* and then *The X Factor*.

But off-screen he's really nice, totally likeable, and very hospitable.

At our first meeting, I felt he was trying too hard to be a character—the interview seemed stage-managed by his publicist. It began with a gorgeous model stepping out of Simon's front door and excusing herself just as I arrived and continued with pop stars leaving praiseworthy messages on his answering machine as we talked.

He relaxed after that, maybe he liked the article, and I always got a more natural welcome when seeing him subsequently. For some reason Simon has always called me "Trouble" when greeting me. Maybe he does that for everyone or just can't remember my name.

I remember him inviting me for lunch at that palatial L.A. home and tucking into a delicious crab salad prepared by his domestic staff, Ramon and Jesus, while he enjoyed just his staple diet—cigarettes and Diet Coke.

As we talked that day about the differences between, and the delights of, Los Angeles and London, I couldn't help warming to him further and reflecting that we were both living our dream—enjoying in Hollywood what his favorite crooners called *The Good Life*.

GARY OLDMAN

For someone who has played so many memorable and scary villains, it's almost surprising how soft spoken, gentle, and friendly Gary Oldman is.

He's another example of actors being very different in real life from the characters for which they are best known.

There is no trace of the dementedly evil characters he has played in films such as *Bram Stoker's Dracula, True Romance, Leon: The Professional, The Fifth Element, Air Force One,* and *Hannibal.*

He's actually extremely warm, modest, and funny and chatting with the British actor is always a treat.

I remember a story he was telling me about filming one of his favorite roles as Sirius Black in the *Harry Potter* movies and being confused at first why filming repeatedly had to stop—and not just because the child actors were limited by the number of hours they were allowed to work each day between schooling. Here's how he told it.

"If you remember, Ron Weasley had a rat called Scabbers and the rat we were filming with got to take a break every fifteen minutes. We just had to stop for him. Even if the scene was in full flow. It was explained to me that he got tired and we needed to rest. I asked, 'Who's his agent?' I'd like that treatment too."

Film director Peter Chelsom once told me he felt the genius of Gary Oldman was to hide his true self behind wigs, costumes, prosthetics, and accents. So when Chelsom directed him in a 2017 movie called *The Space Between Us* his instruction to Oldman was that he would play a character just like himself and maybe even wear his own clothes. Gary had replied, "Can I at least wear a scarf?"

That was a good movie but not one of his most successful. However, next time out when he disappeared under prosthetics to play Winston Churchill in *Darkest Hour*, Gary had a real "moment in the sun" to use his own words and won for that role the best actor Oscar his talents had long deserved.

MILLIE BOBBY BROWN

One thing that interviewing so many stars has taught me is how to spot special talent.

I instantly know if someone has star quality from the presence and poise they bring to an interview.

When young Millie Bobby Brown became a breakout star from the first series of *Stranger Things*, I wasn't in the least surprised.

That's because I had already predicted it two years earlier when interviewing the then ten-year-old Millie for her earlier sci-fi show, *Intruders*.

I was moderating a panel she was on with her much more experienced and better-known adult costars and it was the kid who had all the best stories and opinions, but not in any kind of precocious way.

Annoyingly, some of the audience were laughing as if they couldn't believe such perfectly formed sentences and well-crafted anecdotes were coming out of the mouth of someone so young.

Her poise was no surprise to me. I've interviewed a lot of child actors and the key is to interview them in just the same way as you would a grown-up performer—and I think Millie responded to that.

After all, they are there to do a job just like the rest of the professionals so why make concession to their age?

Millie was also professional enough to say thank you to me afterward rather than just walking off and blanking you as soon as the interview was over like so many do, such as Julianne Moore who I'd interviewed the previous week.

She also introduced me to her parents who were at the screening and panel interview, and I could tell they were good people too who would make sure Millie wouldn't go off the rails like some other child stars have in the past.

Her acting in *Stranger Things* and other projects is top notch and I'm excited for all the great performances we'll see in the future from Millie Bobby Brown.

THE CHUCKLE BROTHERS

I owe my very short career in stand-up comedy to British double act The Chuckle Brothers.

When I interviewed Barry and Paul ahead of a children's show they were doing at Blackpool's Grand Theatre, they seemed to think I was funny and asked me to open the show for them.

Well I was thrilled because this was my hometown theatre and I longed to be on that stage one day, plus I always fancied myself as a bit of a comic.

Looking back on it now, I realize I shouldn't have been so eager to agree—and should have maybe worked harder on my material.

It's important with stand-up, so I gather, to judge your audience correctly.

I confidently went on stage talking about the shows I had watched on TV the night before. But looking down at the crowd, consisting of around a thousand boy scouts, brownies, and girl guides, they all looked under the age of eight so would have been tucked up in bed before any of those shows came on.

That would explain the blank looks they were giving me as I was dying up on that stage.

A good comic always pivots when they are losing the crowd and goes to their best joke.

I didn't have any, just an offensive one I remembered from school. So I thought I would tell that.

"There were these two Irish fellas on the rollercoaster at Blackpool Pleasure Beach theme park," I smiled.

"As it gets to the top of the track, Paddy turns to Murphy and says, 'Are you sure this train goes to Manchester?'"

Silence.

But then seconds later the whole place erupted into howls of laughter and cheers.

Not for anything I'd done, however.

The Chuckle Brothers had appeared on stage and each stuck a custard pie in my face.

As I staggered toward the theatre wings, struggling to see through the foam which way I was going, I knew I was walking toward my retirement from comedy.

The Chuckle Brothers carried on with the show and brought the house down, as always.

There's a reason they were the ones performing and I was the one interviewing. We all have our talents.

Mine clearly isn't for stand-up comedy. Not for a crowd of young kids anyway,

PETULA CLARK

When you write about celebrities, they are not always pleased with the results. But you are not their publicist or fan club president, you have to objective, call it as you see it, and report the facts.

I pride myself on accuracy, don't misquote anyone, and I am proud to say I've never been sued over a story.

But I've had some stars very unhappy with what I wrote—one example is the late ventriloquist Keith Harris, of Orville the Duck fame, who threatened to push me in a boating lake after I reported his extramarital affair.

I never expected veteran singer Petula Clark to be unhappy with my write-up of her interview with me for a long established and respected British newspaper. Especially as it's the one time I felt I'd used almost too much flattery in a profile piece as I described the *Downtown* singer's remarkable showbiz career.

But I was flabbergasted when she detailed what her objection was. "You have described me in print as 'happily married'. How on earth do you know that I'm happily married?" demanded Petula.

Well, the fact she'd told me that she and her husband Claude Wolff, a publicist whom she married in 1961, were still together and loved spending each summer and Christmas together with their three children and two grandchildren at their chalet in the French Alps painted a pretty happy domestic picture.

But she wasn't having any of it. Sorry to make such a radical assumption, Petula. And I hope everything is ok at home!

PETER CAPALDI

*D*octor *Who* stole my Crunchie.

Peter Capaldi, who was playing the title role at the time, joined his *Doctor Who* costars and producers at San Diego Comic-Con where, prior to their convention panel in front of thousands of fans, they were giving backstage interviews to a small, hand-picked selection of journalists.

I was among the chosen few and sat at a table where one after another the guests would file in and do an interview of exactly eight minutes—I guess when you travel in time like the characters in this sci-fi classic, your timings are precise.

It was a fun assignment for me as I've always loved that show and had met all the other living Doctors, Tom Baker, Peter Davison, Colin Baker, Sylvester McCoy, Paul McGann, Christopher Eccleston, David Tennant, and Matt Smith. Splendid chaps, all of them. I would later meet the current Doctor Jodie Whittaker and found her wonderful too.

The interviews in San Diego were hungry work as I'd done back-to-back chats all day with stars from other shows and films, I'd had no time for lunch and the rapid interview schedule left no time in between chats for a snack.

So I'd brought with me my favorite British chocolate bar, a Crunchie, as a reward to enjoy at the end of my final interview.

It stayed there on the table as I interviewed one guest after another, with my stomach rumbling between chats, until eventually my last interview of the day, Capaldi himself, took a seat.

Seeing a chocolate bar on the table, the star assumed it was for him, picked it up, unwrapped the Crunchie, bit into it, and awaited the first question. What a sense of entitlement stars have to presume food is always for them!

My bottom limp was trembling and my stomach was rumbling, and he continued to tuck into the chocolate treat, completely oblivious to my internal suffering.

All I wanted to say was, "That was my Crunchie, you arse."

Instead I drew on all my professionalism to ask, "What's the most fun thing about playing this iconic role?"

I can't remember the answer—I was too hungry and sad about my Crunchie.

MIKE LEIGH

British film director Mike Leigh is such a misery guts—as anyone who's seen his often depressing films won't be surprised to learn.

I was due to interview him on stage after a screening of one of those movies, abortionist drama *Vera Drake,* which I'd seen a week earlier as preparation.

But he showed up early and sat outside the screening with me while the movie was playing as I prepared my questions and occasionally tried— and usually failed—to make small talk with him, just getting grumpy responses each time.

The strangest thing happened whenever he would notice someone step out of the film to go to the bathroom.

He actually followed them and demanded to know what was wrong with their bladder that they couldn't sit still for the two-hour duration of his film, getting bemused looks and rapid apologies in return.

Then when I introduced him on stage, in very flattering terms, he interrupted me, saying, "Never mind all that" and berated those audience members who had stepped out to spend a penny.

I was his next target after opening with, "I notice you've never cast an American actor in any of your films. Why is that?" I got the response, "What a bloody stupid question."

So I asked if he had a bloody good answer to it and he certainly did— slamming the quality of American acting training and saying it wasn't a patch on British tuition.

Standing up to him seemed to have worked and we got to the end without anybody getting hurt.

But I'm in no rush to interview Mike Leigh again anytime soon.

MATT GOSS

If there was an award for the most well-groomed performer in show-biz, it would have to go to Bros singer turned Las Vegas headliner Matt Goss.

He is a lovely, sweet guy, a huge supporter of charities, and has become a friend. But when I last went to visit him at his Vegas home I had to fit in my visit between house calls by his masseuse and his personal hairdresser.

Matt came to the door in a silk robe revealing waxed legs and chest.

His face was smothered in fake tan and his eyebrows were perfectly plucked, plus he looked to have curled his eyelashes.

I'd never felt so unkempt!

Later that day I even bought a self-grooming kit.

In case you're wondering, the beauty show wasn't for my benefit—Matt had a concert that night. And it was a belter.

But I'm not sure how pleased he must have been with his haircut because he wore a hat on stage throughout the show.

PAUL ROSS

've appeared on so many TV shows over the years, usually as a "talking head" giving opinions or insight on celebrities, but one glorious day I was a game show contestant.

The show was called *Tellystack*, a short-lived TV trivia contest, and the host was one of my favorite broadcasters, Paul Ross.

But I felt sorry for Paul that day because I ruined his show—by knowing the answer to every single question.

I felt even sorrier for the other two contestants because if there's one thing I know about, it's television trivia and I soon built up a huge lead.

Worried that viewers would be switching off due to a lack of suspense, I would hold off from pressing the buzzer even when I knew the answer so I could give my opponents until the last possible second to answer it first and catch me up. When they didn't, I'd come in late with the answer.

I make no apologies for building up my points total because I really wanted the first prize for the show's highest scorer—an all-expenses paid trip to New York.

Weeks later I was in the Big Apple and it was a glorious visit in a lovely hotel with everything paid for.

Paul obviously had no hard feelings because he worked with me again on another even shorter-lived game show called *Psychic Challenge*.

The idea was that three psychics would try and guess the identity of a celebrity guest through a series of psychic clues like reading their star chart or holding one of their possessions.

But due to low ratings the show got quickly cancelled—something even the psychics didn't see coming.

Although I've been on his radio show several times, Paul has never had me back on one of his TV shows since and that's probably very wise. They get cancelled so quickly that I'm obviously bad luck.

SACHA BARON COHEN

The world now knows Sacha as the mischievous comedy genius behind outrageous comedy characters like Borat.

I first knew him as the quiet guy in the corner at the production offices of Talk TV, a London cable television station, where I was part of the presenting team on an entertainment news series called *Showbiz UK*.

One day he wasn't there and when I enquired as to his whereabouts I was told he had gone to the Edinburgh Fringe Festival.

"Oh I didn't know he liked watching comedy," I said.

"Watching it? He's performing it," came the reply.

That seemed ridiculous as Sacha barely spoke to anyone, let alone told jokes. I guess it's always the quiet ones.

But clearly someone at the station spotted his talent because he was hired to copresent the fledgling channel's anarchic youth series, *F2F*.

Watching those shows was like seeing a star born—Sacha completely came to life on camera and first started formulating the comedy characters which would later make him a star.

Talk TV was great fun. I loved working with host Andrea Boardman as well as guest hosts Natasha Kaplisnky and Jerry Hall and interviewing the celebrities on each show. I have fond memories of author Jackie Collins, who told great stories, and less fond ones of magician Paul Daniels who I liked not a lot.

I would go on to appear in well over one hundred TV shows but Talk TV was my training ground and I thought it would last forever.

But very suddenly it was gone. Sacha and I and the rest were out of a job. All because of the death of Princess Diana.

On August 31, 1997, all our programming was replaced by Sky News coverage of the tragedy.

It never came back on—the whole channel was closed down a week later and that was that.

We all know what happened to Sacha since as he deservedly rose to become one of the world's top comedy acting talents.

It was exactly twenty years later when I saw Sacha Baron Cohen again—in Mexico of all places.

I was due to interview him there on stage at the international press launch of his latest movie.

Recognizing me instantly from the Talk TV days he greeted me with the words, "So, I see you got another job then."

CHAPTER 5:
SANDRO AND MORE STARS

HUGH JACKMAN

No one tells a story like Hugh Jackman.

He's such fun company and his tales go in really unexpected directions.

To show you what I mean I'll tell you the following in his own words after I asked Hugh how helpful it had been to consult with illusionist David Copperfield in preparation for his role as a magician in *The Prestige*.

"So helpful. David took me to his secret magic museum in Las Vegas. It's actually underneath a sex shop....

You go to the back of the store, find a blonde mannequin, press her left tit, and a secret door opens.

Then down the stairs, you switch on the light and he's got a treasure trove of magic history down there, like Houdini's water cabinet and all manner of great stuff. Just being around him and all those great illusions was a huge help with getting into character."

Shortly after that I went to Hugh Jackman's birthday party—which was a wonderfully over-the-top song and dance performance extravaganza.

He opened the night with a great line I've adapted myself at similar celebrations, saying, "Welcome to the party. I'm forty-five tonight or, as we say in Hollywood, thirty-seven!"

SCARLETT JOHANSSON

When I learned I was going to interview Scarlett Johansson on my birthday, I couldn't have been more excited.

It seemed like the best birthday gift of all time from the universe because I'm such a fan of her acting and her looks.

Determined to make an impression on my Hollywood dream girl, I went out to the local party supplies store ahead of the interview and bought a giant button—or badge as I used to call such things in Britain—with the words "Birthday Boy" written on it.

My hope was that Scarlett would see it, read the words, smile, lock eyes with me, fireworks would go off in her head, and she'd fall instantly in love with her devoted fan.

But expectation and reality are often so different.

Scarlett walked in, greeted me politely like the professional she is, then squinted her eyes to read what was written on my lapel, and said quizzically, "Birthday boy?"

I replied, "Why, yes, Scarlett. Today is my birthday. And I get to spend it with you. What do you think of that?"

She simply said, "Whatever."

The interview then proceeded as normal and that was that.

Guess we won't be sending out the wedding invitations just yet then.

PARIS HILTON

When I learned I was to copresent an award with Paris Hilton at a Hollywood awards show, I was determined to make it slick, fun, and special.

There was just one problem.

I would have to speak my lines in Chinese.

Because these were Chinese film industry awards held in Hollywood and the majority of the audience spoke Mandarin.

Not a problem. I have a few Chinese American friends and persuaded one of them to teach me a few lines that I could remember and hopefully pronounce properly.

I stepped out on stage and Paris invited me to speak first.

I delivered brief remarks about the importance and significance of strong ties between the Chinese film industry and Hollywood, discussed the best producer award we were about to present, and thanked everyone for coming.

Rather than applauding my efforts at Mandarin, everyone in the sellout crowd just looked at me blankly.

Was it my poor pronunciation? Did I misunderstand cultural differences? No. They were just star struck by my cohost.

Seconds later I introduced Paris Hilton and the place went absolutely nuts.

She didn't speak Mandarin. In fact all she said on the microphone was, "Hey!"

Nevertheless, Paris's one word greeting got a standing ovation.

I couldn't compete with that.

MICKEY ROURKE

One meeting with an acting idol that went perfectly well was when I finally came face-to-face with the eccentric, extraordinary, and unforgettable Mickey Rourke.

His self-destructive tendency had derailed a career that seemed so promising after early films like *9 1/2 Weeks* and *Angel Heart,* and he had languished in the movie wilderness until a remarkable performance in *The Wrestler* reminded the world of his talent and sent him onto the Hollywood awards circuit—where our paths would finally cross.

I was so pleased to be interviewing the unpredictable enigma on stage for an audience of film award voters and the star certainly didn't disappoint.

Moving with a tough-guy swagger and shaking hands with sausage-like fingers, he showed up with his pet Chihuahua and a large entourage which included action star Jason Statham, model Lisa Snowdon, and wrestling legend Rowdy Roddy Piper.

Mickey was flamboyantly dressed as usual. I was too—which prompted him to greet me with the words, "Have you been raiding my closet?"

When I introduced him on stage moments later, the large crowd got to its feet giving a deafening ovation and sweet affection to a talent who was only now getting the recognition his ability deserved.

Then he related a comeback tale to me and the audience so compelling—about an actor beaten down by life but looking for a return to the big time—that I knew it had to be told in a book. I was inspired to spend the following six months researching and writing my first biography, *Mickey Rourke: Wrestling with Demons.*

Friends of the star told me so many fun Mickey stories, from the time he set his home on fire trying to cook his own dinner to the occasion when the tough-guy actor and one-time boxer cried his eyes out while getting his ears pierced. But they also stressed how he dragged himself up from the cinematic scrapheap to win respect and awards.

They say you should never meet your heroes in case they disappoint you. Mickey didn't. And I hope I did justice to his inspirational story.

ADAM SANDLER

There are some movie stars who are totally different in real life than their usual on-screen persona. And then there's Adam Sandler.

Off-screen, he's just as affable and casually dressed as his comedy movie characters.

Happily, he's just as funny too.

Adam has a way of lifting spirits at the best of times but he made me smile at one of the worst.

Shortly before interviewing him and his costars for *Grown Ups 2*, I'd been in a hospital after taking a nasty fall and I turned up for our chat on a walking stick and still in a lot of pain.

I got through it somehow and he and the rest of the cast, Salma Hayek, David Spade, Kevin James, and Taylor Lautner, were pleasant enough but only Adam checked in with me later to make sure if I was ok.

But rather than turning it into a gooey, over sentimental moment, he made it more comfortable by making fun of both my speaking voice and the way I was limping like a certain Dickensian character.

In a deliberately bad English accent he asked, "I've got a question of my own ... will there still be goose for Christmas, Tiny Tim?"

Thanks for making me smile Adam—and thanks for the entertainment.

I interviewed him again for his most recent film, at time of writing, *Uncut Gems*, and wow, what a great performance that was. Highly recommended.

BEN AFFLECK and JENNIFER LOPEZ

've got a lot of time for these two stars—both very friendly, approachable, and fun.

Jennifer Lopez is a real laugh and down to earth—I suspect all that diva stuff was made up by her manager to make her more interesting to the press.

Ben Affleck is very similar but has a really big head. I don't mean he's an egomaniac, I mean he really does have a large head.

They seemed a perfect couple and when they were together romantically they got so many headlines but it didn't seem to me like there was much love there.

I learned a lot by watching them closely at the premiere of the flop film they made together, *Gigli*.

Ben and Jen worked the red carpet expertly, as a perfect double-act holding hands and answering all questions together with good humor.

But as soon as they reached the end of the red carpet and went inside away from the cameras, they parted without even looking at each other and went off in separate directions to spend time with their respective friends.

They only came back together for the exit photos outside.

It taught me a lot about Hollywood and made me skeptical for a while about various other celebrity relationships.

EMILY BLUNT and JOHN KRASINSKI

One showbiz couple that clearly love each other and are great fun to hang out with are actors Emily and John.

But every relationship has potential roadblocks and John shared an amusing one with me while his wife excused herself from our chat at L.A.'s Bel Air Hotel about the film they had both worked on, *A Quiet Place*, to go to the bathroom.

He asked me, "Do you watch *Peaky Blinders*?" I confirmed I had seen the British crime drama series.

"Great isn't it? Emily and I watch it too and love it. But there's a problem."

John explained that while Emily had been out of town, he had skipped ahead and watched a few more episodes but hadn't told his wife and she'd said to him earlier that day she was looking forward to resuming watching the series with him that night from where they had left off. But Netflix shows you what episodes have been watched and he didn't want to be found out.

His question was: how could he get his Netflix screen not to show that he'd already watched the next three episodes?

I told him not to worry because I had a Netflix executive on speed dial. I quickly called her up and explained the problem while keeping an eye out for Emily's return.

My friend explained to me she only produced Netflix shows and didn't know how to nobble the on screen menu so, just as Emily returned, I had to give John the "sorry I can't help you" look with my eyes.

Maybe he confessed or they overcame the problem because I saw them again just a couple of weeks later and they were as happy as ever. And they've got good taste—*Peaky Blinders* is a terrific show.

TOM FORD

The fashion designer and filmmaker is the only person to have sent me flowers after an interview.

And I'm not talking about a bunch of dodgy daisies and daffodils lifted from next door's garden.

These blooms were so spectacular, expensive, and perfectly arranged that they wouldn't have looked out of place at the Chelsea Flower Show.

The generous gift, along with the accompanying note, was a touch of class—and perhaps even an apology.

Because when he had turned up for our interview a couple of days before, Tom Ford had barely said hello when he laid out to me a whole list of topics he didn't want to talk about at our interview, which was to be televised.

I just smiled and reassured him it would be fine—and asked all the questions I was planning to ask anyway.

You can't allow yourself to be bossed around like that. He was probably just nervous. But there was no need to be.

Interviews are an information and opinion exchange and the subject can choose to answer questions or not and the interviewer should always be polite and informed, or at least that's my view of things.

Tom soon relaxed into it and told fascinating stories about his life growing up in Texas and his move into acting, then fashion, and now film—he wrote and directed both *A Simple Man* and *Nocturnal Animals* brilliantly.

When I got in touch with Tom just before writing this book, he said he had enjoyed our interview but wasn't so pleased when he saw the filmed version of it—because the lighting was so bad it made him look old.

Let's do another interview soon Tom, without the cameras.

But next time, maybe send me one of your suits as a thank you gift— they last longer than flowers.

JEFF GOLDBLUM

It was one of those gloriously sunny days in Los Angeles when any sensible person would wear a t-shirt and shorts.

Not me. That's not my look. I wore a suit. Always do whatever the weather. But at least it was a linen one.

Going for a stroll on a deserted country lane in my white linens I felt I looked like Alec Guinness in *Our Man in Havana*, a reference for older readers there.

I'd not seen another soul pass by for ages until an SUV with blacked-out windows came roaring past.

Then a strange thing happened. The car came to a sharp stop. Then reversed back to where I was standing. And the driver's side window rolled down.

There, looking at me with the same sense of wonder with which he had first gazed upon a dinosaur in *Jurassic Park*, was eccentric movie star Jeff Goldblum.

He seemed to be struggling for the right words as he sized me up. Then he delivered them, smiling.

"More people should wear linen," he said.

And then he drove off.

A typically bizarre, but a very Goldblumian encounter.

JULIA ROBERTS

The *Pretty Woman* star has become known as "the $20 million smile." But each time I've encountered her she's tended to have a grimace on her face.

Frosty responses in Q&As, stone faced at parties, on her guard at award shows, I've only seen her laugh in movies—all very frustrating as I love her work.

Maybe it's me. Or does she only smile if you pay her $20 million to act? It's probably just me.

I decided to seek the opinion of director Garry Marshall who directed Julia in both *Pretty Woman* and the other movie she made with Richard Gere, *Runaway Bride*.

During a fun interview with him over dinner, the moviemaker said Julia was generally a sunny presence but had her downbeat moments, especially when filming *Runaway Bride*.

He revealed that Julia and Richard were squabbling on the set of that movie—he wasn't quite sure why—and had even given up talking to each other or even looking at each other by the time they came to film the key scene which showed their characters blissfully in love.

That presented a problem for Garry but it's one his wife Barbara solved with an idea for a swift script rewrite.

The big moment shows their characters running and smiling while flying kites. Watch that romantic scene again and you'll notice the screen couple look up at the kites a lot but never once look at each other.

Garry is no longer with us but left some great movies and TV shows behind which will be enjoyed forever.

However, perhaps his greatest achievement was making a romantic comedy film with two stars who had fallen out with each other!

Incidentally, I live just steps away from the Beverly Wilshire, the hotel where the characters played by Julia Roberts and Richard Gere stayed in Pretty Woman.

The movie put that hotel on the map but it was not the first choice location for the film.

Garry Marshall told me the three most expensive hotels in Los Angeles were approached first but they all refused because the script was about a prostitute and all of those ritzy establishments claimed, "we don't allow hookers on our property."

That statement might come as a surprise to anyone who has been in the bar of any of those hotels on a typical Saturday night!

SUSANNA HOFFS

When I saw the brilliant lead singer of The Bangles in concert and met the smart and warm-hearted Susanna Hoffs afterward, my mind immediately went back to what her band's biggest hit, *Eternal Flame*, had meant to me.

It meant I nearly had to go to Arizona and have sex with old women in return for immortality.

Allow me to explain....

I was briefly an investigative reporter back in England and was sent on an undercover assignment to infiltrate a brainwashing cult called Eternal Flame which was preying on British students and conning American investors.

It was run by some Las Vegas hypnotists who were ultimately convicted for their scam, which involved convincing their followers and financiers that eternal life could be created by erotic couplings between youngsters in northern England and senior citizens in the southwest of the USA.

Trying to gather evidence against these con artists, I donned robes and attended one of their prayer meetings in Liverpool posing as a college student feeling lost and looking for guidance.

I must have looked convincing, and not given any clue that I had a recording device hidden under my robes, because the leader picked me out at one point and asked me in front of the crowd, "Can you feel the power of the eternal flame, my brother?"

I couldn't feel it. But I'm sure he heard the loud click of a tape under my robes as it reached the end of its recording capacity at that very moment.

Everything in the room froze.

I then saw a look of confusion then recognition on his face which changed to steely determination. Presumably not wanting to be rumbled in front of his worshipers, he moved onto someone else in the crowd and I took my opportunity to slip away, walking toward the door, and breaking into a run.

Very quickly I heard a cry behind me of "Get him!" I ran as fast as I could and didn't look back.

Robes were flapping in the breeze as I got outside, I raced past dismayed shoppers and passersby and, glancing round, could see three men chasing me.

Using my local knowledge, which I thought the Las Vegas crew would not have, I ran toward the nearest crowded place—Albert Dock shopping center—and tried to lose myself in the crowds.

It wasn't the first time I had been chased as an investigate reporter, so I used a tactic that had worked before—running into the ladies toilet and hiding myself in a locked cubicle.

Two hours later I emerged. With no sign of the Nevada con men's goons, I grabbed a taxi straight to my newspaper's office and handed to my boss the tape, which ultimately helped the police investigation which closed down the cult.

Every time Eternal Flame comes on the radio now, I thank my lucky stars for being a fast runner back then and that I didn't end up on a plane of guys being trafficked to Arizona.

JAKE GYLLENHAAL

I always enjoy a "Caine-off" with Jake Gyllenhaal.

If you don't know what that is, it's a battle of dueling Michael Caine impersonations.

Jake does a great one—and so do I.

We discovered this during an interview for his film *Prince of Persia*.

It started with me doing the classic "You were only supposed to blow the bloody doors off" from *The Italian Job*.

He came back with "Would you like me to get the Batmobile, Master Bruce?" Clever—a reference to Caine's Alfred the butler character in *Batman Begins*.

I thought I'd taken the title with "She was only 16-year-old," a line from lesser known but then recent Caine film called *Harry Brown*.

But Gyllenhaal battled back with "Ruprecht, do you want the genital cuff" from *Dirty Rotten Scoundrels*.

Hard to top that one.

I don't believe Jake has ever worked with Caine, although his sister Maggie has, but he's a huge fan of the veteran British actor.

So am I.

When I met Caine, on the promotional tour for one of his great books, he was just as warm, witty, and wonderful as I'd imagined.

I didn't treat him to my impression of him though.

I just break that out for Jake.

BURT WARD

As you may have gathered over the course of this book, the thrill of meeting a celebrity is much bigger if they are someone you have been a fan of since childhood.

And Zap, Pow, Thwack, what a thrill it was to have Burt Ward guest on my podcast, *Who's the Best?*

I loved watching him and the late Adam West as *Batman* and Robin in reruns of the classic 1960s TV series.

And I loved learning that Burt is now something of a superhero in real life—but to dogs.

He runs the world's biggest rescue foundation for great danes and other large dogs, *Gentle Giants*, and told me, "These days I call myself the Canine Crusader!"

Turns out Burt and his wife Tracy have rescued and rehomed more than fifteen thousand four-legged friends and at any one time have fifty rescue dogs living with them at their California home.

As a big animal lover myself, I was really impressed with that and pleased to find he uses the platform provided by his cult icon status to urge fans to care for dogs.

Holy animal welfare! He really is a hero.

TOMMY LEE

I would never be a good rock star. I'm just not wild enough for the lifestyle. I'm the sort of person who instead of trashing a hotel room would tidy it up before leaving.

Perhaps that's why I've always been fascinated with bad boys of rock like Tommy Lee—the Mötley Crüe drummer and ex-husband of Pamela Anderson whose life has largely been defined by excess.

I was excited to get to talk to him for a short-lived talent search TV series he was judging called *Rock Star Supernova*. But instead of agreeing to meet me at the TV studio, he had a very different plan in mind.

I got a note to be outside a church in the Silverlake section of Los Angeles at midnight where I would receive further instructions.

By half past midnight, I was feeling cold, sleepy, and vulnerable and, tired of waiting, was about to head home when a minivan pulled up and a guy in the back opened the door and said, "Sandro? Jump in. Let's go see Tommy."

So I did.

I had no idea where I was going but it was with a sense of relief that a few minutes later we stopped outside a lavish hilltop mansion and I was shown inside.

Walking through the main house, which was full of beautiful people, I enquired, "Where's Tommy?" I was pointed in the direction of the outdoor swimming pool.

There, chatting with fellow rock stars Gilby Clarke from Guns n' Roses and Jason Newsted of Metallica, was the man himself.

Drinks appeared and soon I was chatting with Tommy who turned out to be a great storyteller, total gentleman, and perfect host.

Despite the environment of booze and beauties, there was no wild antics that night, just a really elegant vibe and a nice atmosphere. Maybe I was a calming influence.

I was due to meet up with Tommy again after the next year's MTV Video Awards but it never happened as he got thrown out of the event earlier in the evening for having a violent fight with Kid Rock.

Now that's more what I call rock n' roll.

ARNOLD SCHWARZENEGGER

The Terminator titan is a larger-than-life figure in many ways and always seems to have a performance aspect to his personality. It seems he's never not "on."

But he's also very smart and calculating, qualities which helped him succeed in politics and rise to become Governor of California

To demonstrate what I mean, it was interesting to learn that his professional rivalry with Sylvester Stallone was very real at one time and not a media invention. Although they were business partners in the *Planet Hollywood* restaurant chain, both were determined to outdo the other at the box office.

Remember when Arnold successfully became a comedy star as well as an action star thanks to smash hits *Twins* and *Kindergarten Cop* and Sly wanted to follow the same route?

Well there was a terrible script doing the rounds at the time called *Stop Or My Mom Will Shoot* and Arnie planted a fake rumor in the press and industry that he was determined to star in it. He suspected that Stallone would think this comedy movie must be great if Arnold was chasing it as his latest comedy triumph.

Arnie's instincts proved correct, Stallone insisted his team acquire the project and when the movie came out it bombed badly giving Sly one of his biggest flops and stalling his comedy ambitions.

They get along much better now by the way and whenever I meet either of those action icons, it's always an incredible experience.

MICHELLE WILLIAMS

Four-time Oscar nominee Michelle Williams is a terrific actress but she had very little confidence in her performance as Marilyn Monroe.

She told me so as we sat backstage, literally behind the screen, at the first public showing of her film *My Week with Marilyn*.

Michelle confessed she'd been surprised to be offered the part, thought she was wrong for it but had worked really hard to get it right and yet was worried how it would be received.

So it was a beautiful thing to witness her sheer relief and joy as she heard the laughter, applause, and cheers coming from the audience watching her movie.

And the standing ovation she got when she walked out on stage with me afterward was so very well deserved.

I'm something of a Marilyn scholar and expert—seeing as how I wrote and directed a hit play and audiobook about the icon, the previously mentioned *Marilyn and Sinatra*, and produced a Los Angeles revival of the stage play version of her hit film, *The Seven Year Itch*. Take it from someone who had researched and studied Marilyn Monroe closely, Michelle Williams captured her perfectly.

GEORGE CLOONEY

You'd think most people would be honored if you named your pet after them. Not George Clooney.

Days before interviewing him on stage at 20th Century Fox Studios in Hollywood I'd rescued a stray cat from a shelter who needed a home … and a name. As he was grey haired, middle aged, and handsome, I naturally called him Clooney.

When I related this story to the other Clooney, he screwed up his face and said, "A cat? A cat? Really."

But then George's tastes in domestic pets have long been a little strange. He lived with a pot-bellied pig, Max, for eighteen years.

His love for that hog was blamed for ending at least a couple of his relationships. George Clooney's ex-girlfriend Celine Balitran reportedly gave him the ultimatum, "It's the pig or me" and he picked the pig.

By the way, pigs are hugely intelligent and entertaining. So too is George.

Apart from his feelings about cats, he's the best company and one of the most charming, likeable people in showbiz.

LEONARDO DI CAPRIO

A big name with a heart of gold, Leo doesn't get—or seek—enough praise for the charity work he does to make life better for others.

Case in point, we were chatting at a Hollywood party and when he asked me what I was working on, I told him I was supporting a fundraising campaign to build a movie theater in a deprived area of South Los Angeles where the kids have to travel for miles on a bus if they want to attend a cinema.

The idea was to use film to bring the community together by installing a cinema in a local park and I added we were tens of thousands of dollars away from success but were determined to see it through.

The next day Di Caprio sent a check for the remaining funds needed and soon after that the screening room was up and running—and most people who used it would have no idea who their benefactor was.

Not unless they are reading this that is.

I'd always been impressed by Di Caprio's acting talent but his class, generosity, intelligence, and social conscience are just as special.

NEW KIDS ON THE BLOCK

I'm too young to have experienced Beatlemania but I can't imagine even the crowds for the Fab Four were as frenzied as those for New Kids on the Block on their first major UK tour.

I got to follow the American boy band on the road reporting their every move and my ears are still ringing from the piercing screams of their fans.

The lads themselves were all great—with the possible exception of Donnie who didn't seem as amused as his bandmates with some of the stories I was writing about them.

I got my love of headline writing on that tour. When a loose bit of wood scaffolding fell on Jordan it was 'New Block on the Kid'. When Danny got diarrhea it was 'Poo Kid on the Block 'and when Joey got the same illness the next day I went with 'New Kid on the Loo'.

Now that's what I call creative writing. Thanks for the inspiration lads.

I got to see their show every night and what a slick entertaining operation it was—catchy songs, terrific dancing, and impressive vocals. Every one of them was talented.

It's so remarkable and pleasing to see them still performing together now—and still getting the same screams, if not the same over-the-top newspaper headlines.

MORGAN FREEMAN

If you were to ask me who was the most boring star I ever interviewed, then the answer would be easy: Morgan Freeman.

It's a shame because as an actor he's electric—just think of the deep-voiced dynamo's work in *The Shawshank Redemption, Seven, Glory, Driving Miss Daisy, Unforgiven,* and all the rest.

But off-screen, a total snooze, at least to me.

I just couldn't get him to say anything interesting at all, despite using all my interviewing experience to try and open him up.

In semi-despair, I asked Morgan what he liked to do to let his hair down, something that would really surprise people.

He replied, "I like puzzles. I can sit with a word puzzle for hours."

Wow, how the long nights between movies must just fly by.

Nothing wrong with being dull of course, but when you've got readers or an audience to entertain there's a duty to come up with something worth reading and I felt like a failure as an interviewer after meeting him.

TOBY KEITH

"Every cowboy sings a sad, song song" and I apparently sang the saddest of all on a visit to a cowboy karaoke bar in Las Vegas.

Finding myself in gambling gulch on a Monday night I realized there wasn't as much to do on the Vegas Strip then as at the weekend, which probably explains why I wandered in to such a place.

Country singer Toby Keith, whom I'd briefly met once and was really nice, gave his name to the establishment but he wasn't there that night—which is probably why they let the likes of me on stage.

Now, I enjoy a bit of karaoke as much as the next show off, but my usual go-to songs—*Welcome to the Jungle* by Guns n' Roses and *Sweet Caroline* by Neil Diamond—were not available in this bar as it was only for county music songs.

Looking through the selections in puzzlement, the only song I vaguely knew, having heard it on the radio a few times, was *Where Were You (When the World Stopped Turning)* by Alan Jackson.

The only lyrics I remembered were the chorus, something like: "I'm just a singer of simple songs, I'm not a political man, but I watch CNN."

Well, I've been on CNN a lot so I thought I could bring some insight there. And, as a born ham, maybe I could bring some comedy to the performance and entertain the rather lifeless crowd gathered in the bar that night, especially if I could create the right atmosphere.

So as I stepped on the stage, I stuck the straw from my drink in my mouth like a hayseed, plunged my thumbs into my belt buckle, and immediately felt like a country singer.

As the music started, not really expecting such a slow tempo, I started dancing about and smiling to the bleaker than expected lyrics appearing on the screen.

When I sang the line "Where were you when the word stopped turning" and improvised a "yee-haw" after it, the booing started.

I thought that was unfair so I doubled down by making an attempt at line dancing while singing along with the lines "Did you sit down and cry?"

Cries of "Get him off the stage" started up then. It entered my head that this was the difference between Britain and America. Back home, karaoke was all about putting on a show and entertaining the crowd. Here they clearly expected a voice good enough for *Nashville's Next Great Star*.

Anyway, before I knew it and long before the song had finished, I was hauled off the stage, thrown out, and told to come back when I'd learned some respect.

Bit harsh I thought.

Until it was explained to me later what that Alan Jackson song is all about.

Turns out it's a poignant tribute to the victims of the 9/11 attacks.

Oops.

And, knowing that now, yes I do feel awful about what happened.

Sorry to Toby Keith, Alan Jackson, and especially everyone who was there that night. I'm an idiot.

CHAPTER 6:

AS FOR THE REST...

There are so many more stars I've met that it would need an extra volume to get to them all—and maybe that's an idea for the future.

But for now I shall sum them up in a few brief words below in the hope I haven't left out your particular favorite.

Before I go down the list, let me stress something you may have learned while reading these stories. Stars aren't always, or even often, what you expect them to be like judging from their public image.

Sometimes they are. But in my experience, it's not always wise to judge a book by its cover.

Talking of books, I wrote one about COLIN FIRTH, called *The Man Who Would Be King*, after meeting that charming actor and learning he wasn't a mirror image of the characters he's played. If you were to assume he was like the roles he's best known for—kings, aristocrats, and successful businessmen, you might expect Colin was born with a silver spoon in his mouth and raised in an English mansion. But, coming from a family of globetrotting teachers and missionaries, he spent much of his childhood in Nigeria and St. Louis, Missouri. On returning to school in England, he was bullied because of his American accent but acting class, the only class he excelled in by the way, helped him both speak like his fellow Brits and find a path in life.

ANGELINA JOLIE may have an ice queen image sometimes but that's unfair because she's very smiley and funny. To see her throw her head back and laugh uproariously, as I have, is a joyous site. But no, it wasn't at one of my jokes.

HOWARD STERN is super shy. That's why he wears sunglasses a lot to stop people looking him in the eye. In my view, this radio star is one of the best interviewers in America, but when I interviewed him he seemed very nervous to be on the other side of the desk. Lovely polite guy though. EDDIE MURPHY is another contender for shyest star. He and Howard have such big personalities but as is often the case with the loudest voice in the room it masks a quiet side. And while we're about it, PIERS MORGAN is a professional provocateur but has always been polite, lovely, and encouraging whenever I've met him.

I'm still often guilty of prejudging celebrities. IAN McKELLEN I somehow thought would be a total "luvvy," trotting out endless actor-y stories with him as the hero. Wrong again, Sandro. He is a great storyteller but is a lovely and friendly person too and not ego-driven. His friend PATRICK STEWART used to be a lot more "up himself" especially in the *Star Trek: The Next Generation* days, but over the years has become much less uptight, much more relaxed, and at peace with his place in the showbiz firmament and is now one of the sweetest stars to interview.

LADY GAGA seems very vulnerable but so caring. A real wears-her-heart-on-her-sleeve type. I was so impressed when meeting her while she promoted *A Star Is Born*, a role Gaga admitted she doubted she could pull off. But what a performance.

GOLDIE HAWN is great company, a sunny presence, and also a great inspiration. She has been underestimated her whole career but has constantly risen above other people's expectations. Starting out as a go-go dancer, she rapidly achieved her dream of Hollywood stardom, remained at the top, and became the first major actress to produce as well as star in her own movies. She's devoted so much of her time to making the world a better place through charity work and always uses her fame as a platform for good.

EDDIE REDMAYNE is another you really warm up to. It's like he hasn't got a mean bone in his body, the guy is just a force of light. Always enjoy chatting with him.

TARON EGERTON is very similar. Like a perfect best mate. Although I don't know him as well as Eddie and Taron, I get a very similar feeling from JAMES CORDEN.

NICOLE KIDMAN has never given a bad performance and never given me a bad interview either. I'd say the same about CATE BLANCHETT. Both are ace actresses who have stayed at the top of the profession for years and also retained their ability to tell entertaining stories.

TOM HANKS always appears to have a lot of "gatekeepers" around him, meaning each interview seems to need more preparation and planning than with several other stars, but once you get to speak to him, he's terrific, funny, and upbeat.

You can see why KEIRA KNIGHTLEY is a star from the moment you meet her—she has a smile that lights up a room. That illuminating grin was needed when I interviewed her on stage in Hollywood once when the lights in the theater went out and I had to interview Keira in the dark.

JENNIFER LAWRENCE is insanely likeable and goofy. I remember her saying in one of our interviews, "The answers to the questions seem so clear and clever in my head but then I open my mouth and all this shit comes out." Don't ever change, Jen.

RYAN GOSLING is really cool, very polite, and extremely laid back. Not as laid back, however, as CHRIS PINE who was almost falling asleep when I interviewed him. I don't think it was my questions that sent him to sleep though as he looked like he was recovering from a rough night.

TYRA BANKS is a tough cookie. She treated our interview like a chess match that had to be won. Suspicious of every question, she would claim that one question was a set up for something that was coming later and one soft question was designed to get her to open up before I followed up with a much more personal one as if I was setting traps for her to fall into. And in each case, she was absolutely right. Tyra must have had really good media training or developed uncanny instincts. Good for her.

OLIVIA COLMAN is just the same in real life as she is in her acceptance speeches at awards shows—funny, cheeky, and self-deprecating. Indeed a brilliant actress and wonderful company.

WILL SMITH is another with whom what you see is what you get—positive, smiling, engaging. I'd add though that unlike a lot of stars, he understands that interviews are a big part of stardom and an opportunity to get his positivity across. Therefore, Will seems to prepare for them with all the diligence he would bring to an acting role, bringing new, fun stories every time.

NICOLAS CAGE and JIM CARREY are both as eccentric in person as you expect. They probably have a dark side like everyone else but I've only ever seen them both upbeat.

MATT DAMON is super down to earth. I checked into a hotel at the same time as him once and he not only turned up with no entourage but insisted on carrying his own bags so he didn't put anyone to any trouble. Although I have noticed that whenever he's around George Clooney he loses all maturity and regresses to a snickering fourteen-year-old. Those two together are like *Beavis and Butthead*.

VIGGO MORTENSEN is another no frills, no fuss, super down-to-earth guy—and a brilliant brain as well as a brilliant actor. I've got a lot of time too for JOAN COLLINS, what a remarkable life she has lived, and there are a few better places in the world to be than sitting next to her hearing her showbiz stories.

BILLY CRYSTAL has played a special part in my life. The first time I was ever on a movie set was when I worked as an extra in a film of his called *Forget Paris*. He's been the best ever host of the Oscars, an event I've covered for over twenty years and always loved. And when I finally got to interview him, he was completely loveable and hilarious.

HARRISON FORD is as iconic as he is laconic. He seems to carry his fame so effortlessly and meeting him is a strange experience because he's been such a part of all our movie going lives that it's almost like he isn't real. But Harrison is human like the rest of us. He just seems superhuman to me. But not as approachable as his *Star Wars* costar MARK HAMILL who still has the enthusiasm of a teenager and despite spending much of his movie career in outer space remains resolutely down to earth.

Another very familiar face in all our lives is JENNIFER ANISTON. I'd seen her in so many episodes of *Friends* and countless movies too, so ended up greeting her like an old pal when she was promoting her Apple TV+ series *The Morning Show*, even though I'd never met her before. Luckily, she must be used to that and was extremely pleasant.

As for the most horrible to me, no contest there—ROSEANNE BARR. She acted utterly nasty and hate-filled around me. That mean streak cost her big time in the end when racist, repugnant tweets got her sitcom pulled from the air.

Of all the stars I've met, the best communicator and most intuitive is OPRAH WINFREY. It's hard to explain but she just gets you and everyone else. Spending time in her company is like being with a psychologist, a teacher, a President, or a pope.

The most inspirational is director DANNY BOYLE. He started out sweeping floors and driving trucks and through sheer hard work and talent ended up directing fantastic movies like *Trainspotting, Slumdog Millionaire*, and a more recent favorite, *Yesterday*.

The best teacher would be RICHARD CURTIS, writer of *Yesterday*. I went to one lecture on writing by him and it unlocked so much in me. He was very self-deprecating claiming that with *Four Weddings and a Funeral, Notting Hill*, and *Love Actually*, he was just writing the same movie every time but I don't buy it for a second. Those movies have so much heart—and so does he.

The most strong, or maybe I mean authoritative, is CHARLIZE THERON. She's so tall and carries herself in such a no-nonsense manner that you automatically feel a tough and commanding presence when she's in the room. No wonder she was so convincing in that *Mad Max* remake.

Of the many other pop stars I've met, my favorites to chat with are TONY HADLEY from Spandau Ballet who is hilarious with brilliant stories, CHESNEY HAWKES who is full of heart and humor, and ANITA POINTER from THE POINTER SISTERS who is outspoken and outrageous.

Thinking back to the stars who are no longer with us, JOAN RIVERS is the one I miss most. She could always raise a smile in person as well as on-stage or on-screen.

The funniest star I've interviewed is KATE BECKINSALE. Her sense of humor is off the charts hilarious in person and watching her Instagram videos every day always makes me smile.

Of all the writers I've met, the one I've got the most time for is the screenwriter of *The King's Speech*, DAVID SEIDLER. He has a great sense of humor about the business and the writer's place in it. I remember him telling me that the day after he won the Oscar for that script, he was summoned to a Hollywood studio meeting and thought he was going to be offered a fortune to write whatever he wanted next. Instead he found four of the previous winners of the best screenplay Oscar were at the same meeting and they were all asked to pitch against each other for the chance to get a job rewriting one of the studio's dud scripts. He didn't get the job.

One of the great survivors of the business is ANGELA LANSBURY. She starred in the first movie I ever saw in my life, *Bedknobs and Broomsticks*, and it was incredible to chat with her when she was a guest speaker at a big journalism awards ceremony in Los Angeles three years ago. The *Murder She Wrote* star consoled me after I was nominated but failed to win the Entertainment Journalist of the Year Award. She said, "I've been nominated for an Emmy seventeen times and do you know how many times I've won? Zero! You'll get over it." I certainly have.

I feel like such a winner to have met all these great Hollywood stars.

And to get to attend such amazing events like Comic-Con, the Oscars, movie premieres, and countless parties. Going from Blackpool to Beverly Hills has been quite a journey and proves that childhood dreams do come true.

Interviewing, reporting on, and meeting Hollywood stars has been, and continues to be, the privilege of my life.

I must confess, there truly is no business like show business.

The End